Rewild Your Home

Bring the Outside In and
Live Well Through Nature

VICTORIA HARRISON

Photography by Maria Bell

Hardie Grant

QUADRILLE

Introduction 6

INTRODUCTION

Nature has an undeniable ability to lift our spirits, and spending time outside can refresh our minds and soothe our souls. From wild swimming and forest bathing to wildlife gardening, more and more of us are tuning in to the benefits of a wilder lifestyle.

But does this connection have to end when we move indoors? While we can appreciate the advantages of being outdoors, it's somewhat surprising to learn that, between work and home, we now spend on average 90 per cent of our day inside. We may have no option but to spend such a large amount of our time indoors, so I believe these spaces deserve to be as healthy, supportive and natural as possible.

In order to find a way back to a wilder way of life, I wanted to see if 'rewilding' our living spaces and decorating with natural materials, colours, shapes and textures could have positive benefits for our health and happiness. By digging into the science of how nature and happiness are interwoven, I set out to explore how biophilic design (the concept of bringing nature indoors) could help reduce stress, improve mood and reduce our impact on the planet.

WHAT IS BIOPHILIC DESIGN?

Biophilic design is the idea that bringing nature into the home environment can improve health and wellbeing. Popularized as a term in the 1980s by Edward O. Wilson, it's since been adapted as an architectural practice where it can be used to measure and shape the way we build new homes in order to make them more connected to the natural world.

Many of the ideas in this book dovetail into this biophilic philosophy. Increasing natural light, maximizing outside views and using natural colours, textures and patterns are all pillars of this design practice, and all have shaped the ideas in this book.

By using these architectural standards as a jumping off point, I've created a sourcebook of design and styling ideas to give you practical, easy ways to retrofit your space and weave in little layers of wild with whatever budget you have.

URBAN LIVING

This desire to reconnect with the natural world and rediscover the simple pleasures of 'wild' living is not a new concept. Many of us instinctively feel the connection between nature and health. We are drawn to natural colours and textures and are soothed by the sound of flowing water and birdsong. We are, after all, part of 'nature' ourselves and our natural habitat is actually a much wilder one than many of us experience today. Just 200 years ago – a flash in the evolutionary timeline – only 7 per cent of the world lived in an urbanized area. Fast forward to today and more than half of the world's population lives in urban areas and this number is growing fast.

The impact this has had on our homes has been startling. New-build homes are packed together in increasingly close proximity, shrinking in size, with more light and noise pollution, and many without direct access to gardens or any real visual connection with the natural world.

The landscape around our homes has drastically altered too. Since the 1930s, we've lost 97 per cent of all wildlife meadows in the UK and the World Wide Fund for Nature estimates we could also be losing 10,000 wildlife species every year. We're greying our green spaces at an astonishing rate, and by closing up our homes, paving over our gardens and taming our landscape in this way, we're losing our vital link to the natural world.

RECONNECTING WITH NATURE

It's no wonder many of us long for a reconnection with nature. So how do we go about redressing the balance? The good news is there are lots of small, easy changes we can all make, wherever we live, to feel more in tune with, and part of, the wild outdoors.

By 'rewilding' our living spaces and decorating in a natural and sustainable way, I believe we can start to bridge the gap between indoors and out, bringing positive benefits for the environment, as well as boosting our health and happiness levels.

From growing edible houseplants to making light maps and maximizing wild views, this book will look at fun and creative ways to link your living spaces to the outdoors. Each chapter will help you breathe fresh life into your home and encourage you to build your own wild habitat, weaving in a little sunlight, starlight and nature as you go. There are quick creative projects sprinkled throughout and plenty of ideas to inspire, whether you live in a rented urban apartment or a larger family home.

There are also ideas for rewilding the outside of your home, wrapping it in greenery and flowers, offering refuge for native wildlife and making it beautiful for your neighbours and passers-by. Many of the ideas and projects will also, in turn, help to support and protect the environment outside your window.

Organized in bite-sized topics, you can dip into a specific chapter to get targeted ideas and advice as required or you can just read it right the way through. Whatever your requirements and desires, all the ideas, tips and suggestions in the book are designed to help you achieve a bright, welcoming home with nature at its heart.

FOLLOWING THE RESEARCH

In piecing this book together, I drew on several scientific studies and design theories, all of which are listed on pages 186–188 for your own reading. From studies into materials to the importance of plants indoors, plus the architectural discipline of biophilic design, the evidence is out there that we need nature as much as nature needs us. Many of these studies are still developing and new research is emerging all the time, so it's a fascinating field to follow. I've also included links to some of the charities and organisations that are acting to preserve and protect our wildlife and the natural world from the effects of urbanization.

1

WILD
SHAPES

If you take a walk outdoors and look around, you might notice a peculiar fact – there are very few straight lines in nature. If you cast your eye over a 'wild' view, I'll bet the only straight lines you'll be able to find are man-made additions, such as fences, electricity pylons, walls or rail tracks. If you were able to take those modern-day elements away, you'd get an entirely different picture. Once you start looking, you'll see that you're surrounded by soft curves and flowing lines. From the gentle arc of a tree branch to the meandering course of a woodland stream, nature has a way of softening, twisting and curving any hard edges away.

Our homes, however, are often the exact opposite of this. If you look around the room you're currently in, the chances are you'll see neat lines, straight edges and square shapes everywhere. Much of this is for practical reasons – square boxes are easier, cheaper and quicker to construct than curved homes, square windows are more practical than round ones, and so on. But it's a startling contrast and departure from the shapes of the wild outdoors. When you think about it, it's a distinctly 'unnatural' environment to spend so much time in.

But does this matter? Can the shape of our surroundings really impact on our wellbeing? In a word, yes. Studies have shown that humans respond much better to 'biomorphic' shapes (i.e. shapes resembling the curving, irregular form of a living organism) than non-biomorphic shapes. We are soothed by curved lines and stressed by sharp edges. This is entirely logical when you consider that we lived in the wild, surrounded by 'natural' shapes, for thousands of years before we moved 'indoors'. Even a few hundred years ago, our homes would have been built from natural materials such as wood, clay and straw, and as such, they would have followed natural forms and curves and would have been pleasingly wonky and soft around the edges. Modern building techniques have almost totally eliminated this, and today the majority of us live in square, straight-lined boxes. And while this might be economical, straightforward and cost-effective from a construction point of view, it's not necessarily the best environment for humans to thrive in.

While you might not be able to change the shape of the home you live in, what you can do is think about the shapes of the furniture and décor that you place within your home and make choices that reflect the curves and spirals of the natural world, bringing the wild landscape indoors.

HOW TO BRING IN WILD SHAPES THROUGH YOUR DÉCOR

You don't need to eliminate every single straight line to rewild your home, but breaking up some of the bigger shapes and bringing in organic curves will really help to make a difference. Here are a few easy ways to counterbalance straight lines with curved décor, followed by more specific room-by-room ideas.

CHOOSE A LIVE EDGE

Any piece of wooden furniture with a live edge will bring a lovely sense of the wild into your home. This means an edge that has been left as it was found naturally, without being planed and straightened; in other words, a totally unique wobbly edge. Search out live-edged dining tables and coffee tables, and even little wooden stools, all of which bring a direct sense of the outdoors in with their natural shapes and lines. Some even have dips and holes in the surface of the table, smoothed out but left visible, while others may have these filled in with resin to create a uniform surface. Any piece of live-edge furniture will provide an immediate connection to the outdoors, as well as showcasing the skill of the craftsperson who made it. On a smaller scale, you can also buy live-edged wooden bowls and chopping boards which make a lovely addition to a kitchen.

CELEBRATE VINTAGE

In the search for pleasing organic shapes, it can often pay to have a look around vintage shops or flea markets as vintage furniture can be found in beautiful shapes. Bow-fronted sideboards or dressing tables work well in a modern apartment, as do some of the more stylized pieces of wicker furniture from the 1970s, such as curved cane chairs. Barstools or chairs with softly curved spindle backs will add lots of character to a kitchen or dining room. Antique closets can be more aesthetically pleasing than modern ones too, especially if they have a gently curved top or delicately carved legs. Vintage mirrors often have lovely curved shapes and etched surfaces too, and collecting a few of these to hang in a group on a wall can make a really pretty feature.

WARM UP WITH TEXTILES

Textiles can work wonders to soften the edges of a sharp-edged room. Round rugs can serve a double purpose of softening lines visually, as well as adding a tactile layer of comfort underfoot. Try placing a circular rug underneath an angular sofa or armchair or next to your bed to add a curve to a linear room. Circular shapes also work well in children's rooms, so try a brightly coloured round rug under a bed or as a playmat. Round cushions are great for adding life and movement to straight-lined sofas and beds too; choose soft materials and plump fillings and pile them up for instant comfort.

SOFTEN YOUR WINDOW FRAMES

Window treatments are another easy way to soften hard edges. Natural cotton or linen curtains have a lovely drape and if you choose an open weave, the threads of the material will show through too, bringing a gentle sense of organic movement.

Blinds and shades can also be softened with a trim along the bottom edge to bring in a natural curve; a scallop trim gives an elegant finish, or a pompom trim adds movement to a blind in a child's room.

Another way to bring in wild shapes is through curtain tie-back hooks. Look for hooks in natural shapes such as shells or leaves and use these to draw curtains back from the window in a curved drape.

ADD MOVEMENT TO A WALL

Woven textiles really come into their own here, and you can use these to introduce natural shapes to break up an expanse of straight wall. A woven wall hanging will liven up an uninspiring wall and add movement and texture too – look for hand-woven wool or cotton textiles in gentle, natural colours. Round wall-hung mirrors in natural materials, such as rattan or wood, are another way to bring a sense of movement into your home; search out those with interesting shapes, patterns or textures.

NATURAL ARTWORK

Artwork is another great way to bring in interesting shapes; look for botanical motifs or floral shapes to bring in curves and spirals. Photos or paintings of nature can also provide soft shapes for your eyes to rest on, whether you choose rolling landscapes or close-up details. Framing is also important to consider, so choose wooden, cane, rattan or driftwood frames for a relaxed, natural look. Collages of pressed flowers and leaves are also a lovely way to bring in the outdoors (see page 100 for more details).

MAKE TACTILE DISPLAYS

Bringing in natural finds to create small, tactile displays is another way to introduce natural shapes. A spiral of polished pebbles or a dish of gathered seashells are pleasing shapes to look at as well as to touch. Anything you find on your travels can help to introduce those lovely organic shapes to your interior. A feather popped into a vase, a piece of driftwood on a sideboard or a dish of polished conkers in the autumn are all little pieces of wild treasure.

WREATHS AND GARLANDS

Circular flower wreaths and trailing garlands of natural materials and shapes also make excellent wall decorations. You can make these yourself (see page 24) or buy ready-made paper garlands of leaves and flowers to loop around picture frames or decorate plain walls.

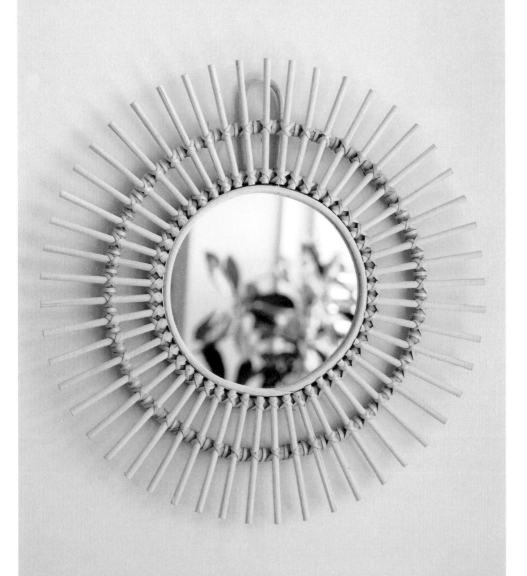

BRINGING IN NATURAL SHAPES ROOM BY ROOM

IN THE KITCHEN

Many kitchen elements are neatly man-made and precise – a wall of storage units, an expanse of neat rectangular tiling, a stretch of glossy laminate worksurface. The materials used in kitchens are often hard-edged too, from glossy cabinets to crisply-edged ceramic tiles which can make this space feel very boxy. Much of this is neatly practical, but a few small additions can really help to make a clinical kitchen feel much softer and more welcoming.

If you have a dining table in your kitchen, choosing a circular or oval-shaped one will go a long way to counterbalancing any hard edges, and if you have an island, choose wooden bar stools with an organic curve rather than angular metal stools. When dressing the table, opt for round placemats and carved wooden utensils.

Live-edged or naturally shaped wooden chopping boards will instantly bring the outdoors in, as will the addition of handmade stoneware storage jars or woven bread baskets. Having some beautiful pieces of crockery on display will also introduce warmth and life to the space, particularly if you choose organic handmade pieces. Fresh herbs in a planter on a windowsill or worktop will also add natural movement.

IN THE LIVING ROOM

Sofas, TVs, coffee tables and storage units are all essential living room components, but these can quickly create a boxy feel, especially in a small space. However, there are a number of quick fixes you can apply and the easiest is to bring in just one or two pieces of curved furniture. If you're in a position to replace your sofa, choose one with a curved back, turned feet or a good level of squishiness to it, rather than a contemporary square-lined style. If you have an existing sofa you want to add curves to, try circular cushions, soft throws over the arms or place a circular rug underneath. Coffee tables or side tables with circular or oval tops are a good way to do this too, as they are easy to add to a room and the curved edges mean no sharp corners to bump into if space is tight. Light fittings can also introduce natural shapes, if you choose fluted or curved pendant shades.

TVs are unavoidably large and rectangular, and can easily dominate a living space, but you can reduce the visual impact by surrounding it with artwork or accessories to counterbalance the straight lines. If yours is wall hung, don't leave it languishing on the wall all on its own – pair it with a couple of wall-hung accessories such as baskets or wall hangings in natural materials and textures to create a gentler grouping of shapes. If yours is placed on a floor unit, group a couple of natural objects around it to soften it and blend it into an overall scheme.

Straight lines are, admittedly, very practical and many of us have boxy storage units, such as cabinets or bookcases, in living spaces. However, you can easily combine practicality with natural style through your choice of materials. If you have cube storage with pull-out boxes for example, opting for boxes made from natural materials like woven seagrass, cotton or felt, rather than glossy plastic, is every bit as practical, and will bring in those softer edges and a more pleasing natural texture.

IN THE BEDROOM

Beds, chests of drawers, wardrobes and closets can be very
rectangular and dominating in a bedroom, but all these items can
easily be softened. If you are able to fix a new headboard to your
bed frame, bring in curves with the addition of a beautiful half-moon
headboard. If you aren't in a position to update the headboard,
cushions, throws and other textiles go a long way to rounding
off any sharp edges, so be generous with these on a bed, choosing
soft, circular shapes and lots of lovely textures.

Built-in storage is, by its very nature, very straight lined but even if
you can't change the shape, you can still have fun with the handles.
Choose nature-inspired styles such as shells, leaves or even animal
shapes, to add an organic, irregular form that you'll have contact
with each time you open the doors. You have more options for
bringing in natural shapes if you are able to choose a freestanding
wardrobe or chest of drawers as you can look for antique-style pieces
with gently curved fronts or arched tops. Just adding one piece like
this will instantly soften the rest of the room.

IN THE BATHROOM

Bathrooms have to be practical spaces, with plenty of tiling, glass
and mirror, but these hard surfaces can feel very clinical, so bringing
in a few softer elements here can really help to warm them up.

If you're redecorating, look for a splashproof wallpaper with
a gentle curved pattern to provide a contrast to crisp tiling or
vertical cladding. Tiling doesn't always have to be rectangular either
– fish-scale tiles are lovely to use in a bathroom as they can introduce
a rounded shape and provide a nod to an aquatic theme.

Accessories can quickly warm up a bathroom too; choose woven
seagrass baskets for storing towels and toiletries, and pick a laundry
basket in a natural material. Bring in a gentle arc with a curved
mirror on the wall, or hang a group of small vintage-style mirrors
in soft shapes.

PROJECT

Make a nature wreath

Foliage and flower wreaths can be displayed all year round, using seasonal flowers or leaves. Fresh or preserved, these circles of flowers, leaves and berries bring an organic warmth to an exterior or an interior and there are so many ways to make them. Fresh flowers and foliage make a lovely temporary display, or dried leaves and flowers will make a more permanent feature.

The delicacy of this wreath means it is better suited to an indoor wall. If you're feeling creative, here's how to make a very simple seasonal wreath.

You'll need:

■ Medium-weight wire (or a pre-formed wire circle, available online or from craft stores)

■ Scissors or garden snips

■ String

■ Dried or fresh foliage/flowers/berries, such as eucalyptus and snowberries

■ Short length of ribbon, to hang

1. Form a circle of wire by carefully bending it around something curved (the diameter can range from something as small as a flowerpot to a larger item like a paint can). If your wire is thin, use a double thickness. Twist the two ends of wire together securely to close the loop. This will create a natural circle, with a pleasing wobble. Alternatively, you can use a pre-formed wire ring for a perfect circle.

2. Starting at the base of the circle, take your first piece of foliage (you'll need a good amount of stem) and twist it around the bottom third, tying it in with wire or string as you go. Leave the tops untied so they can branch out away from the circle.

3. Once you've got a good base of foliage all around the wire circle, start adding in flowers, berries and smaller items as accents.

4. Take the decorative elements up as high as you like, but you might want to just decorate the lower third or half of the circle.

5. Attach a thin wire or ribbon to the top of the wreath and hang it against a wall or on an internal door where it can be admired every day.

2

WILD
MATERIALS

Using natural materials is one of my favourite ways to bring the outdoors in. You can instantly forge a link to the outside in just a few steps and with minimal outlay. It's also deeply satisfying to pull together your favourite materials to create a scheme that you know will make you feel happy, uplifted and energized.

There is a huge appetite now for finding alternatives to plastics in every aspect of our lives and decorating with natural materials very much supports this desire to live in a more sustainable way. As well as increasing your connection to nature, some natural materials, such as wood, have also been scientifically proven to increase human health and wellbeing by lowering blood pressure and stress levels, so I think there's an argument for using wood in every room in the house.

In the winter months when contact with the outside world diminishes, it's particularly important – and satisfying – to surround yourself with tactile reminders of the great outdoors. For those living in cities in particular, your choice of materials will also create an essential connection with the natural world when it is needed the most.

Another unexpected benefit of using natural materials indoors is the scent that these materials provide. The way your home smells can be as powerful a trigger as the way something looks or feels when it comes to building a wild home. Scents bring with them memories, so choosing to introduce materials like jute or seagrass that have the subtle natural scents can ignite a memory, consciously or subconsciously, of being outdoors in the wild landscape.

There is also much beauty to be found in an object that changes and develops over time. We have become conditioned to think that 'new' is good when it comes to interiors and finishes, but the unique beauty of natural materials is that they weather, change and evolve the longer you live with them. A wooden table that's been scrubbed, sanded and loved for decades, for example, will have a beauty that a brand-new steel and glass table will never acquire. When you furnish your home with wild materials, they bring with them a sense of organic growth and change.

This chapter will highlight some of the best wild materials for your home. The materials are divided into five categories – flooring, walls, furniture, textiles and accessories – and at the end of the chapter I'll show you how to combine these to create a fresh and welcoming space whatever your style.

WILD MATERIAL CHECKLIST

FLOORING

Floors are easily overlooked, but your choice of flooring can subtly play into how each room in your home feels and works. From beautifully grained wooden boards to thick, cosy wool carpets, there are so many tactile natural options to choose from. You'll want a mix of flooring in your home, depending on how much traffic a room gets and its usage. In a hallway, kitchen or bathroom for example, hardwearing flooring is a must, so natural wood, local slate or stone or clay tiles are all good options for a tough, moppable floor. In living rooms and bedrooms, texture is important to keep toes nice and warm, so some of the softer natural flooring options such as wool are a good choice here. Choosing reclaimed wooden floorboards is another way to reduce your environmental impact and it can bring a lovely layer of character and life into your home. If you have hard floors, you can layer up soft, natural rugs on top to cushion and soften. Take your pick from these materials:

Wood

The king of natural materials, wooden flooring is warm, textured and full of character. With that lovely visible grain and warm rich smell, wood often works best when it is kept in as natural a form as possible and simply treated with a natural oil or wax to bring out the colour. Solid wood can also be sanded back and re-sealed to prolong its life and to repair any wear and tear. As with any wood product, look for FSC certification before you buy to minimize any environmental impact. Floorboards can be laid in a number of ways to create different effects; try wide planks for a contemporary style or choose a herringbone pattern for a more traditional feel.

Bamboo

Technically a grass and not a wood, bamboo has a lovely finish when used as a flooring material with visible grass fibres running the length of each floorboard. It usually has a warm honey or straw-coloured tone that develops and changes as it ages (the sun can lighten it), so it brings lots of character and warmth to a room and has a smooth, silky texture that's lovely to feel underfoot.

Stone

Tough, hardwearing, with naturally textured surfaces, stone floors will provide a timeless look and can be easily mopped and maintained so they are a good choice for hallways, kitchens and open-plan spaces. Slate and limestone are some of the most common stones and you can choose from a wide colour range, from inky blue-black slates to warm sand-coloured flagstones. Using a stone that is sourced locally is a great way to really anchor your home in the surrounding landscape.

Terracotta

Terracotta is a beautifully warm and rustic-looking flooring material and is often used as part of a country-style interior. Terracotta floor tiles are also a great choice if you're after a hard floor with a visual warmth to it. If you choose tiles with a handmade finish, they will have beautiful irregularities and texture too. The tiles can be laid square for a traditional look, or (if using rectangular tiles) in a brick herringbone pattern for a little more interest.

Jute

A tough vegetable fibre that can be spun into strong threads, jute is traditionally used to make mats, bags or sturdy sacks. Hessian and burlap are other names for the end product of the jute fibre, but jute is more often seen in interiors. As a material, jute is incredibly tough and practical, and makes a really good woven flooring, either a mat or runner, for an area that gets lots of footfall. The woven texture brings in a lovely contrast when used with smoother materials and I love the warm, golden colour of it when used indoors. The smell of jute or hessian is strangely comforting too, particularly when the sun strikes it – like warm hay on a summer's day.

Seagrass

As you might imagine, seagrass is woven from the fibres of a plant which is found growing under the sea. The aquatic grasses are harvested, dried and woven into a sturdy material that has been used in interiors for many years. In the past, seagrass was used as a home insulation and thatching material, but these days it is mainly used for flooring thanks to its hardwearing nature and tactile finish. It has a naturally golden colour with a green tinge and is slightly silky to the touch. As a woven carpet or rug it adds a lot of texture and character to a room and works beautifully in a coastal home where it provides a nod to its watery origins. As a flooring material it is usually left undyed and woven into either a basketweave or a herringbone pattern. Basketweave will create a pleasingly rustic finish while the herringbone can be used to create a smarter feel in a room. Seagrass can also be used for woven baskets and storage boxes.

Cork

As a flooring material cork is not only durable, tactile and warm underfoot, it's also a great insulator, as well as sound absorbing, so it's a good choice for living spaces and family homes. Forget about the cork tiles of the past though – it can now be bought in the form of boards that can be laid like a regular timber floor and can be used throughout the home. It's not particularly waterproof though, so probably not the best choice for wet rooms or bathrooms.

Coir

Woven from coconut husk fibres, coir is an extremely tough and water-resistant material that is traditionally used to make ropes and mats. In an interior, coir works very well as a tough doormat material and the fibres can also be woven into a flooring material. It's very durable and practical, so it's ideal for hallways, stairs and areas of heavy use.

Sisal

Sisal is woven from another tough plant fibre, this time the agave plant. It's hardwearing and has a light-coloured finish that, like coir and seagrass, works well in a hallway if hard flooring isn't an option. Sisal can be dyed, but I think the natural shades are the most beautiful.

Wool

Hardwearing, insulating and soft, wool is a lovely natural material to warm up a room and keep toes toasty. As such, it's perfect for rooms where comfort is key, such as bedrooms or living rooms. It can also be looped, tufted or dyed many different colours to create a wide range of effects, although I think the more natural the colour, the better. Wool rugs can also be layered up on a hard floor to create an extra cushion of warmth underfoot. If budget is an issue, you can buy a piece of wool carpet and have it cut to size and whipped (the edges bound) to create a bespoke rug at less than the price of many off-the-peg rugs.

WALLS

From wood panelling and clay paints to grasscloth, your choice of wall covering can add heaps of character and texture to any room. Whether you want a hardwearing surface in a hallway or kitchen, or a soft texture in a bedroom, the following materials will provide natural beauty and subtle interest.

Wood

Wooden wall panelling provides a lovely natural warmth and can be a really practical choice in a room that gets lots of wear, such as a hallway. A painted finish can be practical, but leaving the natural grain visible can really help to root your home, with the rings and knots of the tree marking it out as something wild and beautiful that was once growing, living and breathing. Using wood panelling behind a bed or as a headboard is another great way to get natural health benefits (see pages 35, 37, 89 and 137), as well as nicely framing the sleeping area.

Grasscloth

Grasscloth is made from strands of natural fibres woven together and placed onto a paper backing that can be used as a wallcovering. It's a beautiful way to bring natural texture and movement to a wall, and it can be dyed many different colours. The fibres are natural, so the overall finish and colour of grasscloth often has subtle variations in it, giving life and movement that regular, flat wallpapers can't provide. As grasscloth is a delicate, handmade material, it's best suited to bedrooms or living spaces where it isn't going to get splashed or marked as it can be damaged more easily than a painted wall. Try it as a feature wall in a bedroom, or use it to create a softer finish in a living room.

Clay paints

A soft, matt paint in a natural shade can bring a lovely, velvety finish to a living room or bedroom and clay paints are a natural way to add colour to your walls. Cathryn Sanders, of Earthborn Paints, explains that most clay paints are manufactured without the use of VOCs or harmful chemicals, so they provide a wash of natural, breathable colour to your walls without polluting the air you breathe indoors. 'Clay paints can also be beneficial to allergy sufferers too as they are less likely to contain harmful emissions' and, she adds, 'they can be safe to use in children's rooms.'

Marble

Cool, smooth and streaked with beautiful veins of colour, marble is pure luxury in an interior. As a splashback in a kitchen or bathroom it brings a cool beauty and is a deeply luxurious choice. Technically, marble should be grouped with the rest of the natural stones, but I've given it a special mention here as it can provide a unique sense of luxury and finish in any interior.

FURNITURE

The furniture you choose to bring into your home will shape the look and feel of your room almost more than any other element. Choosing natural materials here, such as wood or wicker, will instantly ground a room and add to the natural feel.

Wood

Wooden furniture is unique in its ability to grow more beautiful as it ages and as such, secondhand pieces, which can be picked up relatively cheaply, often have much more charm than new pieces of furniture. I have a scrubbed pine table in my kitchen, the surface of which is criss-crossed with lines, marks and scuffs that tell of all the meals, moments and life that have been shared across its surface for several generations (it had another life before it found its way to my house). As well as containing this rich history, it was also considerably cheaper than buying a new table, so if you're decorating on a budget, secondhand wooden furniture is always a good choice. Charity shops, vintage markets or online marketplaces are all good places to search for wooden furniture and many pieces can be brought back to life with a quick sand down and a fresh coat of beeswax or oil.

Commissioning a new piece of wooden furniture is a lovely option if you have the budget for it, and working with a local craftsperson to create something bespoke for your home will be a wonderful investment. Wooden coffee tables, sideboards or bed frames are all good for introducing a tactile warmth to living spaces and bedrooms, and freestanding pieces such as dressers or linen cupboards will add heaps of character to kitchens and bathrooms. Wooden bar stools or chairs will also bring warmth to a kitchen island or dining table.

Thinking creatively and repurposing more unusual items can also help you to furnish your home on a budget. I have a mahogany church bench in my kitchen that I salvaged from a church a few years ago for less than the price of a new bench or set of dining chairs. It's over 100 years old with intricately carved sides and a bible shelf running along the back, and it has a beautiful sense of life and history. The top rail has been polished to a rich chocolate finish that glows with an amber undertone thanks to generations of hands running over it. Repurposed wooden school desks and benches are also great finds if you can track them down and can add charm and interest to your interior.

Rattan and wicker

Rattan is the name of a group of palms, the canes of which are harvested and used to weave into wicker baskets and furniture. Wicker or rattan lends a pleasingly rustic feel to an interior and woven furniture pairs particularly well with country-style florals and warm wools. With the woven surface being pleasantly tactile, this is also a good material for adding texture and interest if the rest of your room is sleekly modern. Retro shapes such as curved rattan headboards and classic 'peacock' chairs are also great ways to bring this material into a contemporary space.

TEXTILES

While a connection to nature is essential, we also need our spaces to feel warm and safe. Comfort is precisely what we crave on cold winter nights and stormy days – think cosy fireplaces and thickly curtained windows. Equally, in the warmer months, lightweight fabrics can help to filter strong sunlight and keep rooms cool on a bright summer's day. Natural textiles can smooth off the rough edges of nature, while still keeping a connection to the outdoors and it's so easy to bring them into a living space. From linen and cotton cushion covers and table linen to wool throws or chunky knitted blankets, look for unprocessed or natural finishes and layer them up generously in bedrooms and living spaces.

Linen

Soft, relaxed, breezy linen is such a lovely fabric for an interior. Used as a bedding material it is beautifully breathable, with an informal crumpled look and a weave that keeps you cool in summer. Vintage linens are also a beautiful and sustainable choice. Naturally-coloured, soft shades of mushroom or stone are relaxing in a bedroom, while bright white linen creates a crisp, fresh finish that maximizes light in living spaces. The open weave of natural linen is particularly beautiful when held up against a light source, so it works well as a curtain or blind, as it becomes softly translucent to let a flattering glow of sunlight through. If you have a bright, sunny living space that doesn't need curtains to block out light, then sheer linen is a lovely choice for a window treatment.

Cotton

Lightweight, soft, breathable and available in almost any colour, cotton has so many practical uses indoors, as an upholstery material, curtain fabric or bedlinen. However, cotton is also one of the most unsustainable materials, due to heavy production costs in terms of water pollution and intensive land use, so it should be used with care. You can help to reduce your impact on the environment by looking for organic cotton or by supporting brands that have pledged to reduce their environmental impact. When buying cotton, choose items carefully and buy with an eye on longevity rather than a quick fix.

Bamboo

As a fabric woven from the fibres of grass, bamboo is a soft, versatile material that can be used from anything from clothes to bedlinen. In fact, when you first see and touch bamboo fabric, the silky finish and fine texture can be hard to match up to the tough material we're more commonly used to seeing. It's naturally temperature-regulating and can have a softer finish than cotton, so is a great choice for bedding.

Wool

As wool is so good at retaining heat, it's the perfect material for blankets and throws in climates where extra insulation is key. Although it can be dyed many different colours, I find that natural tones work really well, such as soft heathers, silvery greys or sage greens. Woollen blankets also look beautiful with several colours woven together in a tartan or check pattern, drawing a sense of the trees, rivers and woods into your home.

ACCESSORIES

You can also weave in lots of lovely natural materials through your choice of finishing touches. If you live in a rented home you can have lots of fun with accessories such as wooden bowls, bamboo chopping boards, terracotta plant pots, knitted cushions or woollen throws. Bringing in natural materials at touchpoints around the home will also connect you to the outdoors each time you use them.

Storage is essential in every room and you can take your pick of natural materials from seagrass to wicker when it comes to small storage accessories. Keep a rattan basket or a selection of cotton or jute bags to hand by the door so they are easy to grab on the way out to the shops. Try wicker storage boxes to warm up a modern interior, or bring in texture with woven hanging plant holders.

Marble can work well as an accent material to add a high-gloss contrast to more earthy textures. Marble-topped side tables, for example, or small accessories, such as chopping boards or coasters, can bring a touch of luxury to a room and only a small amount is needed to make a big impact.

I'm very partial to wobbly plates and bowls. By this I mean handmade, glazed stoneware that has the mark of the craftsman visible in the texture and finish of the surface. The very opposite of mass-produced crockery, a handmade piece of stoneware has a wonderful tactile quality that is a pleasure to use every day. Stoneware can also be glazed with a range of natural, mineral finishes that bring a sense of the outdoors in.

The most versatile of natural materials, bamboo can be used as an alternative to wood to create bowls, chopping boards and small accessories. The glossy, smooth material can be polished and glazed to create a warmly tactile surface, perfect for little dishes to store jewellery, stationery or keys.

PROJECT

How to choose your natural palette

As this chapter has shown, there are so many wonderful natural materials to choose from when decorating your home. Often though, the skill in decorating is knowing what to leave out rather than what to add in. Having lots of different materials competing for attention can create a somewhat chaotic feel. The trick lies in choosing a small collection of beautiful natural materials that all work well together and introducing these elements throughout your house. That way, you'll have a sense of continuity running like a thread from one room to the next, and the materials will really shine. If the materials are local to your area, then even better.

To build your own mix of materials, I suggest choosing one or two from each category below, calling in samples and placing them together to see how they work. How you react to materials is important, so start by selecting all the materials that directly appeal to you, then whittle them down to a carefully curated collection. You can also reflect your local landscape in your choice of materials by selecting those that create a woodland or coastal feel, for example. I've listed a few of my favourite combinations, but you will create your own totally personal and unique style.

Select your materials from the mix chart below (one or two from each category):

Walls
Clay paint / Wood panelling / Grasscloth / Tiles / Marble

Furniture
Wood / Rattan / Wicker

Textiles
Cotton / Linen / Wool / Bamboo

Flooring
Wood / Stone / Sisal / Seagrass / Wool / Bamboo / Terracotta / Cork / Jute / Coir

Accessories
Marble / Stoneware / Bamboo / Seagrass / Jute / Rattan

MATERIAL MIX CHARTS

Here are some examples of material mixes for inspiration. See the chapter on Wild Colours (pages 49–63) for more inspiration.

Coastal

Walls: Whitewashed wooden panelling

Furniture: Light oak

Textiles: White linen bedding / Blue and white wool blankets

Floor: Seagrass matting

Accessories: Driftwood accessories / Green seaglass / Blue earthenware / Seagrass storage boxes

Mountains

Walls: Warm stone-coloured clay paint

Furniture: Weathered oak or pine

Textiles: Cream linen bedding / Blue and green tartan wool blankets

Floor: Slate flooring / Coir matting

Accessories: Wooden chopping boards / Slate coasters / Jute storage bags

Woodland

Walls: Cream clay paint

Furniture: Warm oak or pine / Rattan

Textiles: Spring green linen bedding / Vintage floral cotton cushions

Floor: Sandy limestone / Wood / Jute

Accessories: White glazed earthenware / Wicker storage baskets / Forest green wool blankets

THE GOLDEN STYLING RULE

Opposites always attract, so think about how the materials will layer up together and pick materials that contrast and complement each other for a pleasing look – glossy marble against rustic wood, for example, or smooth bamboo flooring with a thickly textured wool rug. The aim is to create a tactile and practical mix of textures that work well with each other. A room solely furnished with hard-wearing glossy materials will feel cold and uncomfortable, while a room crammed full of soft textures and fluffy layers will be a bit overwhelming. Try to add an element of contrast into every room.

3

WILD COLOURS

From the sparkling tones of the sea to the soothing shades of the forest, the natural world has the best colour combinations and can be an endless source of inspiration. Choosing your colour palette with nature in mind will instantly help you tap into a 'wilder' home.

Often when we think of 'natural' colour palettes, we imagine earthy tones and soft neutrals. While these colours are lovely in their own right – and can make a beautiful colour scheme – a wild colour palette can be so much more than this. From fern green and rose pink to marine blue and sea-foam white, this chapter will look at some of nature's most inspiring colour combinations and show you how to apply them to your own home.

FIND YOUR HOME'S WILD COLOURS

Colour can be very subjective and we all react differently to certain shades because they are often overlaid with emotion and memory. As such, we have to call on our personal intuition and emotional response when it comes to choosing colour palettes.

In order to help you find a path through endless colour options, I've found there's a simple rule to follow. Look outside and search for the tones and shades in the landscape surrounding you. Chances are, the colours that work together directly outside will also work inside your home and some of the best wild homes are those that reflect their native landscape, sit easily and comfortably in their setting and have a lovely flow from inside to outside. Think of a woodland cabin, built from timber and furnished with warm greens and rich browns inspired by the surrounding forest, or a coastal cottage, with a slate floor in inky blue and pale linens in seagull grey.

So the first thing to do when thinking about indoor colour schemes is to take yourself outdoors. Staying inside and contemplating a wall currently painted in standard magnolia is unlikely to fill you with inspiration, but looking to the landscape beyond definitely will. Get outside to your nearest slice of wild landscape and start to really look around you. These colours will instantly give you a palette from which to start, and an idea of how to pair colours effectively.

Wild colour gathering

You might think you know your neighbourhood, but taking the time to really observe it closely will reveal a few surprises. I love this activity as it really allows you to connect to the landscape outside your front door.

Take yourself out for a walk, with the sole purpose of soaking up and absorbing the colours in your local landscape. As you walk, try to find two or more natural colour combinations that you love, for example a straw-coloured bird's nest, with a sky-blue egg inside and a downy white feather; or a dusty pink rose on a fresh green stem. The key is to really look and take note of the ratio of colours to each other to gather inspiration for your room scheme. The bird's nest, for example, could translate into a soft, neutral room scheme with accents of light blue and soft white. Or, a predominantly green woodland with a splash of wild rose could prompt you to consider a room scheme of soft greens with accents of warm pink.

Wild colours vary a lot depending on your location and there are some classic combinations to be found in each type of landscape. Forest colour schemes, for example, are often soothing and restorative, drawing on dark greens and earthy browns, cut through with flashes of pink and red from wild flowers such as lupins or foxgloves. Woodland colours often start from a similar warm, earthy base, but are paired with lighter tones of dappled sunlight, frothy cow parsley and woodland flowers. A coastal scheme, by contrast, generally has a lovely freshness to it, drawing on sparkling blues, gentle misty greys and sea-foam whites, as well as soft, sandy tones. On pages 58–63 you'll find a few of these classic colour combinations for inspiration.

The secret to finding your own colours is to really observe and cast aside any preconceptions about the shades and tones of the world outside your window. If you live by the coast, for example, it can be tempting to assume the predominant colour palette is blue and white, but there are actually hundreds of different coastal colours to be found depending on your location, ranging from warm sandy neutrals paired with turquoise blues and accents of wave-top white and lichen yellow to more rugged landscapes with cooler sea tones of steel grey and deep blue, perhaps paired with the dark greens and browns of the coastal pine forests beyond. All wonderful material from which to build a colour scheme.

To kickstart your own colour search, observe the following:

- Native plants and flowers

- The colour of crops in local fields

- Hedgerow plants and colours

- Local wildlife

- Local trees

- Water (take a really close look at the shades and tones of it)

- Traditional local architecture (to see if there's a predominant material used, for example honey-coloured stone or blue-grey slate)

WHY IS IT IMPORTANT TO FIND MY LOCAL WILD COLOURS?

If you love all things coastal it can be tempting to decorate your home in nautical stripes and tones of blue and white, which is wonderful if you live by the sea and have the kind of clear light that sets these colours off to perfection. However, if you live inland you might find that it just doesn't have the same effect. A bright and breezy seaside cottage works not just because of the seagrass flooring and white and blue palette, but also because of the fresh salty air that blows through open windows, the sound of gulls wheeling overhead and the clear, reflected light from the water below. All these elements tie together to create a home that feels effortless and rooted in place. Equally, warm tones of forest green, soft amber and foxglove pink would look wonderful when these are the dominant colours in the landscape outside your window – they would play beautifully underneath dappled treelight, but are less likely to work well in a bright coastal area.

So by using native colours, textures and materials you can help to anchor your home in the landscape and connect it to the outside, creating a space that feels welcoming and happy. The more an interior reflects the landscape directly surrounding it, the more connected it will feel and the more authentically wild.

FINDING A WILD LANDSCAPE IN AN URBAN SETTING

While the above approach works beautifully if you live in an area of countryside or coast, the task gets a little tricker when you live in a large town or city, as increasing numbers of us do, where the natural landscape outside is not so apparent. But there are always clues to be found and this task becomes more of a treasure hunt in an urban area. Research the wild origins of your town or city and build up a picture of what the local area might have looked like before urbanization. Woven throughout any urban landscape should still be fragments of river or pockets of original woodland, with all their beautiful tones and colour inspiration.

REFINE YOUR COLOURS

Once you've identified your favourite colour combinations, it's time to whittle these down to find a scheme that will work in your home. Try to reduce these to a small but perfectly formed collection of colours to play with. Aim to have between three and five colours to form the basis of your home's colour palette, for example you could have blue, white, sandy neutrals and silver accents. From here you can start to translate these into paint chips and fabric swatches. Collect paint charts from DIY stores, send off for fabric swatches, and start to see how the colours play next to each other.

HOW TO APPLY THESE COLOURS TO YOUR HOME

Once you've identified your colour palette, it's time to apply it
to your home. A simple rule that will help you to do this is the
60/30/10 rule. This is a commonly applied rule in decorating,
which can help guide and direct you when putting together
colour combinations. Put simply, the rule is:

60% of your room scheme will be your main colour

30% of your scheme will be your secondary colour

10% will be your accent colour

This doesn't mean that you will only have three colours in your room,
but rather that 60 per cent of your room will be tones and shades
of one colour (usually a neutral), 30 per cent tones and shades of
another colour (usually bolder) and the remaining 10 per cent will be
something completely contrasting, such as a complementary colour,
a pattern or metallics.

TAKING A COLOUR PALETTE THROUGHOUT A HOME

As with your choice of materials, your choice of colours will have a
much greater impact if you apply a theme consistently throughout
your home, rather than having a different look in each room.
Selecting a small palette of colours that link to the landscape beyond
and work neatly together is the key to success. How might this work
in reality? You'll want the rooms in your house to flow gently into
one another, without any jarring or clashing so using the same main
colour theme in each room will ensure this. But you will probably
want to use different percentages of each colour in each room to
play with mood. For example, if your chosen wild colours are blues,
whites and accents of silver and sand, then you'll probably use
more of the lighter tones in the rooms you use in the morning and
throughout the day, adding the darker tones as accents. Then you
might flip the balance in rooms you use in the evening, with a higher
percentage of the darker tones and accents of paler shades.

Below are a few classic wild colour combinations to help start your own project.

Coastal colour schemes

A coastal scheme has a lovely freshness to it, drawing on sparkling blues, soft misty greys and sea-foam whites as well as soft, sandy tones. Coastal landscapes often have a bright, clear quality to the light too; think of the way the sun glitters as it reflects off water, so silver, glass and metallic accents work well to recreate that mood. Here are three different ways to draw on coastal colours at home:

1

60% Cool sandy neutrals

30% Steel grey and deep blue

10% Accents of foam white and glimmers of glittering silver and glass

2

60% Cool seagull-grey neutrals

30% Marine blue

10% Accents of natural tones, like the colour of a fishing rope, and warm brass

3

60% Warm sandy neutrals

30% Turquoise greens and blues

10% Accents of wave-top white and lichen yellow

Forest colour schemes

Forest colour palettes are deeply calming and restorative, concentrating on deep greens and earthy browns, punctuated with eye-catching shots of pink and red from wild flowers. Warm neutrals will create a base for this look, with rich metallics and glowing amber accents bringing in interest and highlights. Here are three ways to recreate forest colours at home:

1

60% Warm-coloured neutrals

30% Dark green and amber-toned leather

10% Accents of bright foxglove pink and glimmers of warm copper

2

60% Stone-coloured neutrals

30% Dark charcoal grey

10% Accents of rich leafy greens and botanical prints

3

60% Earthy neutrals

30% Pine-needle green

10% Accents of glittering bronze riverbed tones

Woodland colour schemes

Like a forest colour scheme, woodland colours start from a warm, neutral base, but bring in lighter tones of dappled leaves, grasses and woodland flowers. Drawing on the soft tones of wild roses, frothy cow parsley and dappled light falling through a leafy canopy, these schemes are light, soft and uplifting. Here are ways to use these colours at home:

1

60% Warm dappled neutrals

30% Soft hedgerow greens

10% Accents of florals and foxed metallics

2

60% Stone-coloured neutrals

30% Eggshell blue

10% Accents of soft, feathery white

3

60% Earthy neutrals

30% Fern green

10% Accents of hawthorn white and apple-blossom pink

4

WILD
VIEWS

Very often when we spend time indoors, we become inward facing, but the views outdoors are something that can have a profound effect on health and happiness. As well as connecting us to the changing seasons and life outside, according to scientific research, a view of nature can also have healing powers, helping to lower stress levels, boost contentment and even alter our perception of pain. Looking out at nature can also connect us to something bigger if we feel alone or isolated.

In this chapter we'll look at how to maximize existing wild views from your home and how to green up an urban view. We'll also explore the benefits of introducing 'artificial' wild views to supplement real views, by rethinking artwork, accessories and décor using images of nature to compensate where the real thing is lacking.

IMPROVE SIGHTLINES

Let's start with the obvious one. In a small space sometimes it's necessary to have furniture against or close to a window but, if you can, try to keep sightlines and pathlines to your window clear. Often the layout of a room completely disregards the windows. This can mean that sofas and chairs face away from a window, often towards a wall with the TV on it, and consequently anyone spending time in that room will be seated turned away from the outdoors. So start by trying to position furniture so that you have at least a partial view outside when you are sitting down.

DOUBLE YOUR VIEW

Mirrors are an interior design saviour for so many reasons – they can make a room feel bigger, they can help magnify light levels and, crucially, when carefully positioned they can double the impact of a view. If your room has a small window, positioning a mirror on the wall opposite the window can help to reflect the view back into the room so you can see out from wherever you are. Place your mirror at eye level (consider whether you will mostly be standing or sitting in this space) and choose as large a size as possible for real impact. You could also use a collection of small mirrors grouped together to create a patchwork effect that will show little glimpses of the outside.

CONSIDER YOUR WINDOWS AS 'FRAMES'

Start by looking out of each window, thinking of your outdoor space as a series of small pictures when viewed from indoors. If you have a garden or outdoor space it's tempting to consider it a separate entity to your indoor space, but as soon as you start to think of the two as linked, you'll start to create one connected space that seamlessly flows inside and out. This isn't just for houses with gardens either – if you live in an apartment, think about how you could use a balcony or windowsill to create a wild view.

INVITE NATURE UP CLOSE

Once you've identified the views that need a bit of rewilding, it's time to set to work on greening up these areas to create wild vistas you can enjoy from indoors. The first thing to do is to invite nature right up to your window. If you have a garden, you can do this in a number of ways. Start by placing a bird table or bird feeders in front of a window for a connection to the wildlife in the garden. If you provide food, nesting habitats and clean water, birds will come and provide you with so much entertainment as you watch (and listen) to them outside your window.

Placing insect habitats and bee- and butterfly-friendly plants near a window will bring another layer of wildlife closer to you. You can plant native wildflowers directly in front of a window if you have the space, or use pots and planters if you have hard landscaping outside your window. Choose pollinator-friendly plants (see page 180), then sit back and wait for the bees and butterflies to find your window. If you have space for a small pond within your window sightline however, the amount of wildlife you can bring into view will grow exponentially (look out for frogs, fish, herons, hedgehogs etc), as will your enjoyment of it.

If you don't have a garden, you can still plant pollinator-friendly plants in a window box or a planter on a balcony, to invite wildlife up to your window. For more ideas on bringing wildlife closer, take a look at the chapter on Wild Exteriors (see pages 171–185) for more ideas on how to rewild the outside of your home.

REWILD ANY EYESORES

Sheds, bins and storage areas are all pretty uninspiring but functional elements of a garden, and if yours can be seen from your window you'll probably avoid looking out at them. Before you write them off though, all of these can be made a little wilder with some imagination. Climbing plants are perfect for softening the edges of outdoor structures such as bin stores and sheds, creating a living screen to mask unsightly elements by throwing a wild blanket of colour over them. Try growing roses, clematis or jasmine for a scented screen, or introduce ivy for a layer of wildlife-friendly evergreen cover.

A micro green roof is another brilliant way to wild up your view and increase biodiversity in your garden at the same time. While a proper green roof can be a big structural project, a smaller version of a green roof can be used to excellent effect on top of a low garden structure such as a bike or bin store. If the frame can take the weight, a sedum roof or just a simple square planter seeded with wildflowers can utilize an otherwise wasted space and turn a practical item into a mini wildlife reserve. These are particularly effective if you are viewing them from above, such as from an upstairs window or an apartment.

ADD SOME WILD WATER

The glitter and sparkle of water is incredibly relaxing and soothing and the gentle sound of flowing water is incredibly meditative, so if there's any way to bring some water into your line of vision it will really help to connect you to the wild. If you have space for a water feature or even a small pond, this will bring so much life and movement to your view. In a tiny space, or on a balcony, a small bird bath will tick this box nicely. Going outside to top these up in the summer or cracking the ice in the winter are activities that reinforce the indoor/outdoor connection.

GROW A TREE

If you have the space, I'd always advocate planting a tree in a spot where it can be seen every day from indoors. Observing it grow and change with the seasons is a very absorbing activity and watching leaves gently swaying and shifting is innately soothing. You don't need a lot of space to grow a tree; even if you just have a garden patio or a balcony you can usually find a potted or dwarf tree to fit. When I moved into my house I had a tiny scrap of grass outside the front of my home, so I planted a small dwarf pear tree outside my bedroom window to break up the greyness of the road beyond. I now wish I'd planted an entire orchard of them, as the joy I get from seeing it every day is immense. Early in spring it carpets the ground below in white blossom and each autumn it drips with amazing quantities of fruit despite its dimninutive stature.

GREEN UP AN URBAN VIEW

While it's easy to talk about maximizing natural views when you have a garden space to link to, it can seem more of a challenge in an urban area or an apartment without access to outdoor space. But even if you have an uninspiring and distinctly non 'wild' view from your window, there are still ways to improve it and green it.

Consider if there are any elements of your urban landscape that you might have some influence over. If you live in a residential street, is there a neighbourhood committee that you could join, to discuss installing some street planters or wildlife planting? Are there any plans to plant more trees in your direct vicinity; if not, could you campaign for this? How about installing a few local bird feeders or bird boxes? Ask around and see if there are any local groups interested in greening up the neighbourhood or any plans you can get involved with. If there aren't any groups or initiatives local to you, why not start one?

RETHINK YOUR WINDOW TREATMENTS

A natural view can also be enhanced by the window treatment you choose to surround it with. Start by ensuring any blind or curtain you choose is hung well away from the edge of the window so you can raise or pull them right back, rather than letting them cut into window space and reduce the view beyond.

Then think about the view when choosing the colour and material of your window treatments and use these to enhance it (see pages 68 and 73). If you have a leafy, green view from your window for example, you can magnify the effect by choosing a soft botanical motif for your blind or curtains, or by introducing soft green colours near the window via artwork or accessories.

Try to keep windowsills clear too, in order to maximize the view. Apart from plants, which I make an exception for (see below), keep sills free of all other ornaments and clutter, and keep glass and frames scrubbed clean to boost light levels and enhance views.

CREATE A LIVING FRAME

Sometimes, despite all of these steps, it's not possible to fully control the wider urban environment beyond your window, but you can still wild your view by creating a 'living frame' both inside and out.

Firstly, frame your view from indoors by layering up windowsill plants to create a cloak of greenery around your window. Softening an urban view is all about blurring the boundaries between indoors and out, so try to bring indoor plants close to a window, either in floor planters, hanging planters or pots placed along a windowsill. These will create a leafy border around your window and reduce the impact of a grey view.

Then look at framing the view from the outside, either by a window box attached below your window or plants placed directly outside if you have a balcony. A window box immediately beneath a window can instantly liven up a grey outlook, wrapping it in colour and life and you'll have the pleasure of watching flowers and plants

grow and change throughout the seasons. If you plant it up with native wildflowers and pollinator-friendly plants (see page 180) it will provide a bonus effect of also bringing nature right up to your window, so as well as greening your view you'll also be doing your bit to support native pollinators and you'll have the bonus of being able to watch them from an indoor perch. In doing this, you will also be rewilding someone else's view, because any buildings facing yours will reap the benefit of seeing the wildlife on your balcony and, who knows, someone seeing yours might be inspired to do the same themselves.

For more ideas on how to rewild the outside of an apartment, take a look at the chapter on Wild Exteriors (see pages 171–185).

FAKE A VIEW

The 'views' in your home aren't just limited to the views out of a window though; research has shown that even looking at a photo or illustration of a natural scene can have many of the same positive health benefits of looking at a natural view. So if your views outside are limited, you can supplement them by bringing in images of natural views.

Try hanging natural artwork, wallpaper, prints or murals wherever real views are lacking and, when choosing murals or images, consider going large and covering an entire wall for maximum impact. From forest scenes to ocean views, there are so many ways to bring in natural motifs and 'artificial' scenes of nature and these can work particularly well in a small room such as a hallway, bathroom or box room. In my home I have a tiny cloakroom with only one small street-facing window that I had to screen for privacy, leaving the room very dark and featureless. To counteract this, I covered one wall entirely with an oversized botanical wallpaper featuring brightly coloured flowers and foliage and this has transformed it from a small, dark cupboard into a tiny jewel box of colour and life.

Another fun idea for rooms where curtains, blinds or shades are often drawn during the day, such as a bathroom or child's bedroom, is to choose a printed window blind with natural motifs on it, be that flowers, birds or animals, so when the blind is pulled down to block out the view there's still a 'natural' view of sorts.

CREATE INDOOR POCKETS OF WILD

There tend to be a handful of hotspots in any home that we end up spending the most time in, so it pays to think about the views from these areas and try to create little pockets of wild in them. In a living space for example, you might tend to spend a fair amount of time sitting down and facing the wall with the TV on it. In this case, you can easily create a little 'wild' view in this area by bringing in a few plants, hanging an artwork or photo of a favourite natural scene or even decorating with a botanical-themed wallpaper.

Surrounding yourself with lots of nature-inspired reading material is another way to weave the natural world into your indoor life. From gardening books to travel magazines, a few on a bookshelf or in a basket near your sofa can bring a little wild escapism into your every day. The winter months in particular are the perfect time to settle down with books, magazines or novels about the wild world outside your window. Spend the quieter evenings dreaming of distant shores, rediscovering the nature on your doorstep through local guides or immersing yourself in some of the best nature writing.

GREEN YOUR DESK

By far the most 'unwild' element of modern life is the amount of time most of us spend sitting at a desk in front of a computer. While our office environments are largely out of our control, many of us also spend periods of time working from home, so thinking about the position of your home office space can really change the way you feel during the working day.

When space is tight it's tempting to squeeze a desk into a corner, or tuck it away somewhere dark and quiet, so desks often end up facing a wall which can be pretty uninspiring. If you can manage it, siting a desk underneath a window is much nicer and will instantly wild up your outlook. Is there a corner in your home where this might be possible? Perhaps a small table in the bedroom or a fold-down desk in a living space? If you can't look out of a window, then you can try the mirror trick (see page 66) to reflect a view into your line of vision.

If a wild view is out of the question, you can still weave in some wilderness by surrounding your desk with images of nature, whether that's a photo of a beach scene, green woodland or a cool flowing river. By building your own green view in this way, you'll always have something natural and soothing to look at when you take a break from your screen. If you often have your computer on standby during the day, set a nature screensaver too.

Surrounding your desk with plants is another easy way to negate the wires, screens and blue lights that often take over our office spaces. One or two plants will have the effect of greening the space and bringing in natural colour and movement, as well as cleaning the air. Putting plants on a windowsill in front of a desk also has the effect of blurring the boundaries between inside and out and making you feel almost like you're in an outdoor space, which is particularly helpful if you live in an urban area where you can't easily step outside. If your desk is tiny and plants would be a nuisance, try a floor-standing pot close by or a hanging planter above.

PROJECT

Start an indoor nature journal

So you've cleared your window sightlines, positioned your furniture to maximize visual access, added mirrors, brought in plants and hung natural artwork indoors. So far, so good. All these small changes will add natural views to your daily life, offering little glimpses of wild as you go about your work and chores at home. But how often do you give yourself permission to stop and spend time just looking out of the window? And I mean really looking; observing the world outside, allowing your mind to wander? So often when we are indoors we are preoccupied with jobs, children, housework or looking at a screen. But I would argue that carving out a little space in which to sit and look outside – and allowing yourself time to enjoy it – will connect you to nature in a way that will pay you back so many times over. Quietly noticing and celebrating small natural moments like this can have a profound effect on wellbeing by connecting us to something bigger.

As well as tuning you back in to the seasons and wildlife outside your window, looking out at a green view can relax your eyes and help improve eye health, acting as a counterbalance to computer and screen use. Keeping a nature journal from this viewpoint is a lovely way to strengthen your link to the world outside and keep a connection going in all weathers. Here's how (see the following pages).

1 CREATE YOUR OBSERVATION STATION

Although a dedicated window seat would be wonderful for this, not many of us have the space for one and all you actually need is a little perch near a window with a view. This can be a stool pulled up to a kitchen window, an armchair angled to look out of a living room window or even a bench pulled up to a window on a hallway landing. It doesn't have to be fancy, but having a dedicated spot to do this will give you permission to take a few minutes out of your day for a moment of quiet observation and creative activity. You just need a small shelf or storage box nearby to house a few materials with which to observe, then you're all set.

2 WHAT YOU NEED

- A notebook, diary or sketchbook
- Pens, pencils or other drawing materials

Optional extras
- A camera or binoculars
- Books or cards to help identify birds, insects and plants

3 WHAT TO LEAVE BEHIND

This is ideally an analogue activity, so digital distractions such as tablets, phones and screens should be kept out of sight if possible (unless you are using your phone as a camera or for identifying plants or wildlife).

4 HOW TO KEEP A NATURE JOURNAL

It can be helpful to keep any eye on the same things each time you look, as this allows you to pick up on changing patterns – be that colours, trees, birds, the weather or whatever draws your attention and catches your interest. The idea is to allow your mind to relax and plug in to the changing seasons outside your window. There's no right or wrong way to keep a nature journal, you just need to find a method that works for you and brings you joy. Anything that helps to mark the changing seasons outside is a great way to open your eyes and ears to the view, and help you to tune in to nature.

As you spend more time looking out you'll start to notice more and more, from the changing seasons, to movements and habits of wildlife. If you're able to open the window or step out onto a balcony you'll even be able to notice the changing scents and sounds of the world outside. Keeping a note of these observations is a great way to notice even more and is a very soothing, creative activity. Opposite are a few suggestions of things to observe in your nature journal. Pick any that take your fancy, or try something else entirely. The key is to choose an activity that you find relaxing and enjoyable, whether that's sketching, scribbling or note taking.

NOTE

This is also a great activity for kids. Set them up with a little chair and a journal of their own and encourage them to jot down, draw or colour what they see outside the window every day. It'll be fun to look back on at the end of the month or year and it gently encourages an interaction with the outside even on grey and rainy days.

WHAT TO OBSERVE

Here are a few ideas to kick-start your journalling:

■ Draw or observe the flowers and trees from your window as they grow, flower, set seed, shift and change.

■ Jot down sunrise and sunset times and note how the sun rises and falls in relation to your little patch of garden or green space – which trees does it hit first, which areas keep the sun late in the day?

■ Note the colour of the sky and the shape and type of any clouds.

■ Open your window and listen to the sounds outside. If you've introduced bird feeders or insect-friendly planting (see pages 117 and 180), listen to what you can hear from your window and make a note of any positive changes.

■ Track the birds visiting your garden; photograph or sketch them and note their names.

■ Make a note of any birdsong you can hear from your window, using an app to help you identify and learn new birdsong as you go.

■ Make a note of the weather each day. Rather than giving a cursory glance outside to see if it's raining, you might start to notice if it's a soft misty kind of rain or a brisk, refreshing drench. You might open the window and see the way the garden glitters and sparkles when the sun comes out after a spring shower, or you might make a note of the way the colours outside change under a stormy sky.

■ Open all the windows and see what you can smell. On a hot day you might notice the warm smell of sun-baked earth, or after a rainstorm you might notice a different scent as the rain drums up the ground, bringing a clean, spicy freshness with it. It's particularly nice to be cosy and dry indoors while observing this!

5

WILD
PATTERNS

Once you've got the basic building blocks of your home décor in place, you can start to have fun with the details and this is where natural patterns come in. If you've laid the right wild foundations (lots of natural light, soft wild colours and lovely natural materials), now's the time to sprinkle in some wild pattern.

Used carefully, natural motifs can really elevate your space and create a connection to the world outside. Even very subtle natural patterns can provide a subconscious link to the outdoors and keep you connected to your wild roots.

I've grouped natural patterns into five broad categories and it might be easiest to stick to just one of these categories when choosing patterns for your home. Some people have a real bravery and flair when it comes to clashing patterns and styles, and will mix and match with confidence. However, it does take a definite knack to do this well without overloading a room with too many competing elements. I think it's always better to do one simple thing really well, rather than muddy the waters with too many decorative elements. This way you can build up layers of pattern gradually, avoid a visual overload and create a room that works for you.

Keeping to one type of natural pattern will also increase the impact of it in your home. If you love floral patterns, for example, and use these in each room of your home, there will be a recognizable wild thread running through each room. Similarly, if botanicals are your thing and you introduce a little leaf print into each room you'll instantly have a more cohesive feel and it will also emphasize the beautiful wild patterns. You can vary the colour, the type or the scale of the pattern, but if you select them from the same category you'll create a calm, pulled-together home that feels rooted and well designed.

Finally, patterns don't have to be loud and splashy. If you favour a more subtle approach, you can bring in a pattern via a single-toned fabric or voile panel with the pattern delicately embroidered in the same colour as the fabric. Patterns can also be etched into glass panels or window film to create a beautiful shadow effect that reveals itself when light filters through.

FANTASTIC FRACTALS

A fractal is a pattern that repeats itself over and over again, getting smaller and smaller as it does, and these patterns can be found right throughout the natural world. A fern is a great example of this – each branch divides into smaller fronds, which in turn divide into smaller leaves, all of which repeat the same pattern. Other beautiful examples of fractals in the wild are spiral seashells, branching trees, delicate snowflakes and forked lightning bolts. It's believed that fractal patterns are soothing to the human eye, thanks to this decreasing repetition, so they would be a great addition to a wild home. For each category that follows, I'll note a fractal pattern or two for you to consider. Too much of this effect can be a little dizzying though, so I find these are best used in moderation.

NATURAL PATTERNS AND HOW TO USE THEM

1 FLORALS

I absolutely love all things floral, from soft romantic roses (*Rosa*) and sculptural foxgloves (*Digitalis*) to cheerful daisies (*Bellis*) and more stylized flower patterns. The colours and shapes are so joyful and happy, I could fill my home from top to toe with them. The beauty of florals is that there are so many different styles to embrace and experiment with. Some are soft and romantic, others are bold and stylized; all have a joyful energy and optimism to them.

The softer, more romantic florals are good for creating a cottage feel, while some of the bolder floral prints that draw on the graphic style of the 1960s are perfect for bringing energy and fun to your space. There are many fractal patterns to be found here too; just look for large flowerheads that are made up of several smaller flowerheads, such as cow parsley (*Anthriscus sylvestris*).

How to use them

If you need help choosing the right floral patterns for your home, take a look at the colours you've already chosen for your interior, as these will often help you to select patterns. If you're attracted to gentle pastel shades and pale tones for example, then you're probably going to be drawn to floral patterns at the softer, more romantic end of the spectrum. Alternatively, if you are drawn to stronger, bolder colours, perhaps forest greens and bronzes, then you might complement them with a vibrant, stylized floral print with a stronger pattern and brighter accent colour.

Once you choose your style of floral, you can then mix and match patterns from within this family. So, for bright, stylized florals you can pair different colours, scales and patterns within this family. Whichever you fall in love with, you'll find that just bringing in a pop in the form of cushions, curtains, prints or accessories, will lift and brighten up any room and provide a year-round link to the summer.

Floral patterns work very well in a country-style context where they can mirror the flowers outside. So, when choosing floral patterns, try to make a link with the native flowers growing around your home by selecting designs that feature these. But if you want to bring them to an urban environment, they can work beautifully here too; try layering them up with fresh flowers, either in indoor pots, window boxes or on a balcony, to create a wrap-around floral effect.

Vintage floral patterns are another wonderful avenue to explore; have a look online or in vintage shops for swatches and rolls of antique fabrics to find something totally unique.

2 BOTANICALS

More lush and clean-lined than floral patterns, botanical patterns have a beautifully calming presence, with prints ranging from the bold and tropical to detailed anatomical illustrations of seedheads and plant structures. Botanical patterns often work well as subtle carved patterns on ceramics or stoneware, or abstracted out and used as a repeat in a wallpaper or fabric design.

There are plenty of fractal patterns to be found in botanical forms too; ferns are the classic example, but also look at the spiral growth pattern of a succulent or the branching veins of a leaf.

How to use them

Oversized tropical prints will fill your home with a soothing burst of greenery and a calming presence and they work brilliantly when paired with indoor plants. Leafy green botanical prints also work really well in rooms that have leafy views from the window as they neatly mirror and enhance the effect, creating a lovely indoor-outdoor flow. If you want to create this cocooning effect, green up the view outside your window by using potted plants if you have limited room, or shrubs and evergreens if you have garden space.

You can also enhance the impact of a leafy view by using leaf-print fabric for curtains, blinds or shades at a window, which will double the impact of the view and extend the effect of the sightline, bringing it right into your room.

At the other end of the botanical scale, delicate botanical illustrations have a unique beauty and can work well framed as posters and prints. Detailed vintage-style botanical illustrations will bring a quieter sense of nature to your home than some of the tropical prints, so are good for those who prefer a subtler link to the outside. Pair them with soft neutrals and delicate colours for a quiet natural style, or try a botanical-inspired wallpaper design if you want to make a bolder impact.

3 COASTAL

Spiral seashells, soft seaweed, swooping gulls, curling waves – all these soft, flowing patterns and shapes can bring a hint of fresh sea breeze into your interior. As discussed on page 59, coastal colours, patterns and tones work best in homes near the sea, so if you are lucky enough to be in that category, then these patterns would work beautifully for you.

If you're looking for a fractal pattern here, the decreasing spiral of a chambered seashell is a perfect example.

How to use them

Coastal patterns can be very subtle, from the curve of a wave to the spiral of a seashell and as such, they are innately soothing and relaxing to look at. They are a great choice if you don't want to have obvious 'pattern' in your home.

Try a wallpaper or fabric design with an abstract wave to introduce a quiet nod to tidal patterns or choose seabird motifs to bring in a freewheeling coastal beauty. Seashells have beautiful spiralling patterns that work well as an abstract motif too, and these can be featured in artwork or accessories.

Scallop or fish-tail shaped tiles are another beautiful coastal pattern that can be laid in a curve to resemble the shape of waves or seaweed. Like neatly overlapping fish scales or a mermaid's tail, they take tiling to a new level and make a refreshing change from the ubiquitous rectangular tile.

4 INSECTS

Bees, ladybirds (ladybugs), beetles – these tiny foot soldiers of the
wild are often overlooked in favour of more showy members of the
natural world, but their colours and patterns are truly dazzling when
viewed up close. So many insects have incredibly intricate markings
and bright, joyful hues that are just asking to be used as prints and
patterns indoors. Insect motifs are having a revival, as we reconsider
just how important these tiny species are for the planet's health and
survival. Bumblebees in particular are popping up increasingly often
as a motif on cushions, blankets and bedding, and I am all in favour.

How to use them

Insect patterns can work well on a tiny scale, as a repeat pattern,
almost as a fun twist on a polka dot. Wallpapers or curtain fabrics
that feature tiny insect motifs are lovely to use in an interior, as their
reduced size brings in a wild motif in a subtle way.

If your style is a little bolder, enlarged prints and illustrations of
insects or butterflies can also make a real splash in an interior when
scaled up and framed, particularly beautiful jewel-coloured beetles,
which could also form the basis of a charming wild colour scheme.
Look for posters and prints, or even sheets of beautiful giftwrap that
can be framed. I absolutely love old illustrations and prints, and think
they can bring a lovely, bookish feel to a room. Framing them up in
rows of three often looks effective; you can get reproduction prints
or search out secondhand books for their illustrations and frame
individual colour plates.

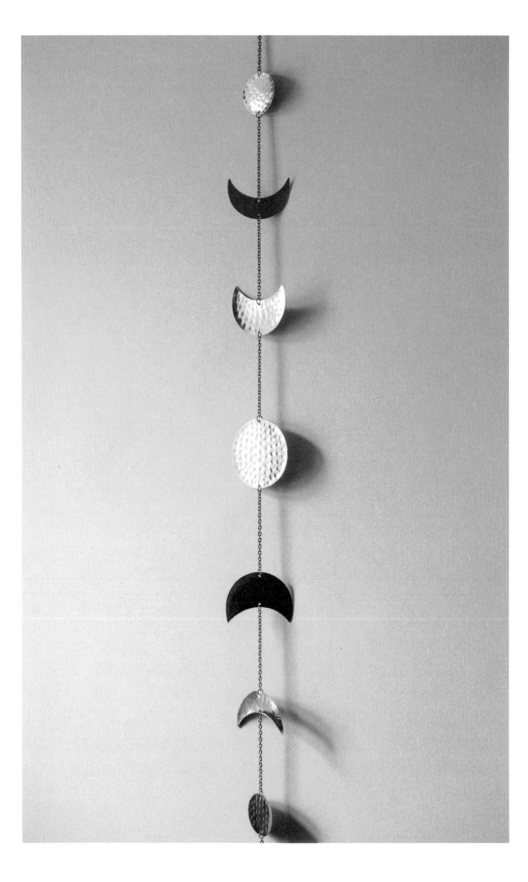

5 THE NIGHT SKY

Stars, moons, planets – astronomical motifs have a magical quality to them and are beautiful to use in an interior. If you've ever walked home late at night under the wash of silvery moonlight and a sky full of stars, you'll know that they have a very special and slightly eerie power that provides a shortcut to the feeling of the wild. When real starry vistas aren't a possibility indoors, astronomy patterns can work beautifully to bring a little of this nighttime magic into your home.

The night sky can be home to fractal patterns too – a forked bolt of lightning is one example.

How to use them

A dusting of stars or a sprinkling of planets can add a link to the magic and calm of the night whenever they are used. Traditionally popular in children's rooms, I think they look stunning when used in other spaces too. Framed star maps are beautiful things in their own right and would look wonderful in a living space or study; the intricate patterns and delicate shapes are very soothing to look at.

These patterns can also work beautifully on the often overlooked 'fifth wall' of a room; the ceiling. Forget those plastic stick-on stars frequently used in children's bedooms, think instead of delicately stencilled stars and pinpoints of gold or silver linked together in star constellations on a ceiling. Perfect for bedrooms, there's something whimsical and soothing about looking up at a night sky and dreaming about the outdoors.

String lights or fairy lights are another way to imitate twinkling little points of light, and they can work beautifully to bring a soft layer of starlight to a bedroom or living space after dark. Look for tiny lights on a very fine wire so they can melt away into the background when they aren't in use.

PROJECT

How to make a botanical-patterned glass decoration

When I was 8 years old, my parents gave me a flower press for my birthday. Like all good presents, it contained within it the possibility of hours of activity and enjoyment. That year it was always in use, preserving all the tiny treasures I gathered from outside. The press itself consisted of two small squares of wood between which you could press anything from individual petals to entire flowers, from leaves to grasses. Your treasures were placed between two sheets of thick blotting paper, then sandwiched between cardboard, placed on the wooden base and topped with the wooden lid, which was then screwed down tight. After a couple of weeks you would open it up again to see how your flowers or leaves had fared.

It was always interesting to see how they transformed in this process, with colours becoming more muted, but shapes becoming clarified. As the tiny flowers became wafer thin and almost translucent, gently peeling them away from the paper was an art in itself.

Flower and leaf pressing is a great activity to get stuck into, for adults as well as kids, as it requires focus to look closely at the tiny details and patterns of the flowers and leaves you preserve. As you reveal the veins, leaves and petals of the items you press, you'll discover beautiful natural shapes and patterns.

This is an idea to create a piece of botanical-patterned glass, which can be hung at a window, celebrating the delicate and beautiful patterns of the wild. It's such a simple and soothing activity and you don't even need a flower press to get started; here's how to create one with just a few materials.

You will need:

- Flowers or leaves

- Thick paper

- Two sheets of cardboard

- A few heavy books

- Small glass hanging frame
(sold in craft shops or online)

1. First you need to select your flowers and leaves carefully. The best flowers, leaves or herbs to press are those with small, delicate stems. Large, thick flowerheads such as roses won't work, so for these you'll need to strip the petals and press them individually instead. Delicate ferns and tiny flower or herb stems are best for this.

2. Layer your flowers between the sheets of thick paper, place these between the cardboard sheets, and finally, place the entire sandwich right at the back of a heavy book. Lay the book flat, place a couple more heavy books on top, then step away and resist the urge to check on your flowers for at least two weeks.

3. After this time, remove the cardboard and carefully peel your flowers and leaves free.

4. Once you have a few flowers that you're happy with, take your glass photo frame and gently sandwich the pressed flowers and leaves between the two sheets of glass. You can arrange as many of these as you like, and in whatever pattern, but often simplicity is best, and just one beautiful shape is all that's needed. Close the frame and hang in a window to admire the shapes and shadows created as the sun shines through.

6

WILD FRAGRANCE

Living in connection with nature means living in step with the seasons and there's no nicer way to do that than by weaving seasonal scents and flavours into your home. Eating seasonally and filling your home with the fragrances and tastes of each season are great ways to stay linked to the world outside.

In spring and summer, it's much easier to feel connected simply by throwing open a window, bringing in fresh flowers and listening to the sounds outside. But in autumn and winter, as light levels lower and days become shorter, it's even more important to link your living space to the world outside and keep that wild connection going. Bringing in seasonal décor and fragrances can act as a daily reminder of the wild world directly outside your window.

NOTE

For each season I've suggested some of the best natural scents for your home. This might be in the form of a scented candle, home fragrance or essential oil. I've included at least one essential oil for each season (marked with '*'), as these can be the simplest and purest way to fragrance your home. Essential oils can also be added to a bath for a seasonal soak.

SPRING

Spring is just the loveliest season, carrying with it the promise of new beginnings, fresh growth, warm sun and the first flowers of the year. There are so many signs of new growth to look out for in your garden and on spring walks, and many ways to invite this fresh, uplifting season indoors. From the first green buds on the hedgerows heralding the end of the winter, to the soft pink blossom on the apple trees promising colour and warmth in later spring, the scents, colours and textures of this season are light, fresh and clean.

At home, spring is a time for opening the windows and doors, polishing windows until they sparkle, drawing in all that lovely spring light and cleaning out plant pots and window boxes for the growing season ahead. This is a season of promise and optimism, and here's how to celebrate and embrace it at home:

WILD SPRING SCENTS

Everything seems fresh and new in spring, and the first colours and flowers to emerge are so valuable after a winter of hibernation. Bright, clean blossom scents will bring that sense of spring freshness indoors, so opt for crisp florals and light, sparkling scents to give your home that spring-cleaned feel. The following room fragrances will weave a spring lightness into your living space.

- Orange blossom
- Bluebell
- Lilac
- Narcissus
- Chamomile*
- Grapefruit*
- Freshly cut grass

THE SPRING TABLE

As the days get brighter and the outdoors starts to beckon, it's a time for lighter meals, with fresh salads starting to replace winter stews. It's lovely to lay a spring table indoors with the first of the season's flowers, a light cotton or linen tablecloth and plenty of light-reflecting glassware. Swap heavy table linens and winter pillar candles for small vases of early spring flowers and a few twinkling tealights in glass jars. As a symbol of spring and renewal, eggs make a beautiful table decoration, either placed in a bowl, or painted and suspended from a vase of branches.

WILD SPRING DÉCOR

Decorate your home with these seasonal treasures to weave a spring freshness into every room.

■ Bunches of daffodils and scented narcissi. Is there any better signifier of spring than a bunch of sunshine-coloured daffodils? Heavily scented varieties are even better – and I like to fill vases and vases with them to properly welcome in the new season.

■ Brightly coloured tulips. Along with daffodils, tulips in vibrant shades are among the first flowers to appear and will instantly bring a vibrant splash of colour and zing to your home.

■ Potted spring bulbs. For a floral hit that lasts longer than cut flowers, potted spring bulbs are lovely to have indoors as they'll often flower earlier than their outdoor counterparts and will give you a headstart on the season. If you plan ahead and plant your bulbs in the autumn, they will be ready to flower very early in spring.

■ Spring flowers in tiny bud vases. If you have them, small glass bud vases are useful for displaying the first delicate spring flowers from your garden or window box. Small glass jars or bottles will do the job just as well.

■ Spring place settings. For a spring table, roll up floral-patterned napkins, tie them with a coloured ribbon and pop in a tiny individual flower stem such as a grape hyacinth (*Muscari*).

SUMMER

Summer is a season of wonderful excess; there is an abundance of colour and life, doors and windows are thrown open to blur the division between inside and out, flowers and fragrance weave their way in and it's a time of heat, warmth and adventure. Coastal finds are wonderful markers of summer, as are bright, bold flowers and strong clear colours. Meals can move outside into the garden or onto a balcony, and tastes and scents get fresher, lighter and cooler. Here are a few ways to celebrate the summer at home.

WILD SUMMER SCENTS

Fresh, clean home fragrances work best in the summer, along with fruity florals. Fresh herbs are another key scent of summer and some of the lighter, cleaner herbs, such as mint and basil, are lovely aromas with which to fill your home. Try the following scents to infuse your living space with the fresh optimism of a hot summer's day:

- Rose*
- Mint
- Strawberry
- Lemon*
- Basil
- Tomato vine
- Peppermint*
- Lavender

THE SUMMER TABLE

Eating in the summer months is a joy. Decorating a summer dining table is all about celebrating crisp, fresh foods and cool flavours. If you can, move a table to a balcony, near a window or outdoors, so you can feast while being cooled by a gentle summer breeze. Gather garden flowers, choose the freshest seasonal salads and vegetables and keep your table decor light and relaxed. Colourful linens, big bowls of salads, pitchers of iced juice and glittering glassware will help you to celebrate this sparkling season.

WILD SUMMER DÉCOR

■ Jam jars or vases full of fresh roses. If you're lucky enough to have space outside to grow a rose, it will repay you a hundredfold. Otherwise, buy a few from your local florist and enjoy their full-blown summer beauty.

■ Bunches or pots of fresh herbs. Herbs can be grown anywhere, from a balcony to a windowsill, and there's nothing better than picking them fresh to cook with. In the summer heat they also give off a beautiful Mediterranean scent when crushed, so choose a couple of your favourites to keep in or near the kitchen for the scent as much as the flavour. Basil, mint and coriander (cilantro) all grow well in pots.

■ Pots of windowsill tomatoes. Growing tomatoes indoors is fun and useful, and I think the smell of tomato leaves is just summer bottled. Tomatoes can self-pollinate, which means they don't need to be outside to thrive, unlike other fruit and vegetables, so they make the perfect windowsill crop. Look for smaller varieties that would grow well indoors, or even a variety that would grow in a hanging basket.

■ Herby place settings. For a celebration meal, roll up brightly coloured linen napkins and tie them with a colourful ribbon and a sprig of scented herb such as rosemary or mint.

AUTUMN

Early autumn/fall is one of my favourite seasons, as the air still has some residual warmth from the summer, but it's cut through with a rich, smoky earthiness. When the light lowers into a golden shimmer you know a change is on the way and the soft morning mists, heavy fruit harvests and warm scent of woodsmoke wind their way through this changeover season.

At home, autumn is a time for productivity before winter sets in. Pickling, preserving, storing fruit and all the last tidying up jobs need to be done before the weather cools off. It's also a time to cosy up – the first occasion to dig out the sweaters, scarves and gloves from the back of the cupboard and layer up blankets on the sofa in readiness for a season of fireside warmth and gentle evenings. As the days get shorter, it's even more important to stay connected with nature and the world outside our door. Here are a few ways to bring the autumn season into your home.

WILD AUTUMN SCENT

Autumn is all about rich, spicy warming scents, laced with a tang of woodsmoke and a rich hedgerow sweetness. To bring a layer of warm, enveloping scent into your home this autumn, try the following fragrances:

- Amber
- Blackberry
- Fig
- Woodsmoke
- Pear
- Apple
- Plum
- Ginger*
- Rosemary*

THE AUTUMN TABLE

After a summer of picnics and alfresco dining, it's lovely to bring the focus back to the dining table and take the time to set it for a meal. In the autumn, textures get heavier and warmer, as casserole dishes and chunky stoneware take the place of light summer salad bowls. Rustic wooden boards are good for placing along the centre of the table and natural forest colours and textures come to the fore. Create a simple table decoration by filling a bowl or jar with pine cones, conkers and wild treasures, layer up textures with linens in autumnal colours and set the scene for long, companionable dinners.

WILD AUTUMN DÉCOR

Decorate your home with spicy fragrances and cosy textures
to celebrate the rich warmth of this beautiful season.

■ Autumn leaves. If you're cutting or pruning branches in your
garden, these make great table displays when arranged in a large
jug or vase. Alternatively ask your local florist to find you some
autumnal colour and celebrate all those wonderful orange, yellow
and copper tones.

■ Wool blankets. Natural wool has a lovely, comforting scent,
so celebrate the warmth and cosiness of this material by layering
up blankets and throws, ready for the cooler evenings.

■ Pumpkins and squashes. Once you've scooped out the inside
for use in soups and pies, carved pumpkins are the best seasonal
decoration in autumn, with a tealight cheerfully twinkling inside.

■ A handful of polished conkers in a bowl. The ultimate signifier
of autumn, these glossy mahogany-coloured seeds are irresistible
to collect and equally pleasing to bring indoors and display, bringing
with them a hint of the warmth and freshness of outdoors.

■ Spiced place settings. To add colour and spice to an autumn
table, roll up natural-coloured linen napkins, tie them with a length
of natural twine and decorate with a stick of cinnamon.

■ Plant pots of bulbs for indoor display. Buy bulbs, such as
hyacinths or 'Paper White' (*Narcissus*), labelled as 'prepared',
and you should have scented flowers by midwinter.

WINTER

There's nothing cosier than being safely tucked up indoors near
a roaring fire while the wind and rain howl outside. During this
season, home is all about creating a welcoming refuge to sit out the
cold weather, but it's important not to get too detached from the
world outside. A little wild weather is just the thing for energizing
sluggish winter spirits, so a brisk walk outside can be a tonic. But so
can returning home to a snug, warm home and watching the world
transform itself outside your window.

This really is the season for bringing in seasonal textures, scents and
foraged finds to keep that connection going to the world outdoors.
Fire is an essential wild element to embrace in the colder months,
and even if you don't have an open fire indoors, lighting a couple
of candles can provide that living flicker of warmth and light when
it's most needed.

WILD WINTER SCENTS

Now is the time to bring out the rich, heady fragrances to wrap
your home in a warming layer of comfort. Spicy scents of gingerbread
and nutmeg have an undeniably festive feel and rich berry scents
are warm and comforting. For the ultimate in festive fragrance,
a pine-scented candle or home fragrance will fill your home with
Christmas cheer.

- Cinnamon
- Clove
- Nutmeg
- Frankincense*
- Berry
- Pine
- Black pepper
- Star anise
- Eucalyptus*

THE WINTER TABLE

Winter meals are all about candlelight, warmth and good company. Taking the time to set a table with thick linens and heavyweight glassware can elevate the simplest of meals to something special. Big serving dishes in the centre of the table for everyone to tuck into make for a sociable occasion on overcast winter days. At this time of year, add in plenty of candlelight to make up for low light levels; church candles placed in a row down the centre of the table are good for bringing a flicker of wild flame to your meal. Decorate with evergreens and bring out your best silverware and glassware to create a glittering, cheerful table.

WILD WINTER DÉCOR

Decorating your home with seasonal foliage can really help you to see the beauty of the winter months. A vase full of evergreen branches and holly berries, or a display of delicate seedheads on a hallway table can highlight the beauty that is still to be found on bright, frosty winter days.

- Evergreen foliage. Wind it around stair bannisters, drape it along mantlepieces and enjoy the rich, resiny scent (see the note on page 122 on foraging).

- Candles. Tap into the elemental comfort of fire by bringing in a living flicker of fire and flame into your home: tealights in glass jars, pillar candles in holders; whatever suits your home. There's something soothing and hypnotic about watching a flame. If you have small children or want to exercise caution about the fire risk, battery-powered candles are an alternative (unscented) option.

- Start sowing spring seedlings. Some spring seedlings can be sown during the early winter months and the act of potting up a tray of tiny sweet pea seeds at this time of year can be very therapeutic, serving as a reminder that spring is on the horizon. I try to have one or two trays on a sunny windowsill and seeing the first green shoots come through while the outside temperatures are still freezing is almost as powerful a tonic as an entire vase full of spring flowers.

- Thick stoneware mugs of hot chocolate. Wild winter is all about recreating the campfire experience from the comfort of your own home. Fill a thick, glazed mug with steaming hot chocolate and enjoy while watching the flickering of a fire or candlelight.

- Wool blankets and thick cotton eiderdowns. Essential for cosying up; choose natural materials and colours.

- Festive place settings. Decorate your Christmas table with thick, cream linen napkins, rolled and fastened with a red ribbon threaded with a dried piece of fragrant star anise.

A NOTE ON FORAGING

I've mentioned bringing in natural finds from your outdoor walks, but I'd like to add a caveat to this. While it's lovely to bring home the odd piece of wild treasure, I feel that foraging should be undertaken with care.

Occasionally, I used to bring home flowers, leaves and berries from walks, but more recently I've found myself conflicted by this and now I generally leave all flowers and leaves where I found them (even those tempting clouds of cow parsley), so others can appreciate them too. Taking anything away from a natural habitat seems counterproductive to protecting these wild spaces. Now I'd much rather leave almost everything as I find it, particularly when it comes to our rapidly decreasing hedgerows and verges.

There are a few things that, in my opinion, are generally acceptable to collect: pebbles, feathers, shells are all usually safe enough to bring home if they are plentiful (but be aware that removing pebbles from some beaches is prohibited, so check local regulations) and if you find a glut of conkers beneath a horse chestnut tree, fill your pockets! But when it comes to branches, flowers and hedgerow treasure, I tend to admire them, then leave them there.

If you want to bring seasonal flowers and foliage into your home, the best way to do this is to grow your own. Even a small windowbox can support an evolving mix of flowers that can provide pollen for bees and insects and seasonal colour for you. If you have a garden, planting one or two flowering or evergreen shrubs will provide you with plenty of cuttings for table centrepieces and vases. Planting your own hedgerow instead of a fence will also provide you with plentiful foraging material, and branches to cut and prune as and when you need them. A hedge can also be much cheaper and easier to install than a fence if you buy bare root plants and pop them in overwinter. And, of course, a good local florist will be able to provide you with seasonal colour and greenery all year round.

For more information on foraging, the Woodland Trust (see page 189) has a very comprehensive guide, along with the guidelines and rules for collecting and cutting wild plants in the UK.

Make your own seasonal room fragrance

There are so many lovely ways to scent your home, from candles to scented oils, but if you want a 100% natural option that's easy and inexpensive, why not try a stovetop potpourri.

Don't let the name deceive you; this is nothing like the dried and dusty potpourris of the past. It's simply a pot of fresh natural ingredients that you simmer in water on the hob to release their fragrance and fill your home with seasonal warmth. You just chop and add seasonal fruit, herbs and spices to a pan of water and keep it bubbling away for a little while to release the fragrance. It's totally natural and is great to make before guests arrive, or for celebration days when scent can play a huge part in creating a cosy and welcoming atmosphere. Just keep an eye on the pot to make sure it doesn't boil dry and, for safety reasons, make sure small children can't reach the pan.

How to make a stovetop potpourri:

1. Slice or chop your ingredients.

2. Add to a pan of boiling water.

3. Reduce to a gentle simmer (with the lid off).

4. Leave simmering until your house is beautifully scented.

5. Remove from the heat.

6. You can re-boil this a few times throughout the day if you wish. It's a good idea to put it on to simmer an hour or so before guests are due to arrive.

7. Once you've finished with it just drain the water and pop the ingredients in your compost bin.

You can add anything you like to your stovetop pot; experimenting with flavours just adds to the fun, but here are a few ideas to start you off.

Sparkling spring

Sliced lemon

Sprigs of rosemary

Summer fresh

Sliced grapefruit

A bunch of mint

Autumn warmth

Sliced apple

Sliced root ginger

Cinnamon sticks

Winter spice

Sliced oranges

Whole cranberries

Pine twigs (cut from a Christmas tree)

Cinnamon sticks

Star anise

7

WILD
LIGHT

Sunshine makes us all feel good. When we're outside we naturally absorb daylight, soaking up its energy and using it, without realizing, to regulate our internal body clock. Throughout the course of a day, as light levels imperceptibly change from the crisp, clear light of the morning to the richer, warmer light of the evening, the type and strength of light sends our body cues to wake up or wind down.

When we're indoors however, these natural light levels obviously drop, making it harder for our internal body clock to regulate itself. And when we start to override these natural light sources with artificial light, things can start to go awry.

So, how do we correct this? A connection with natural daylight and its rhythms is recommended by nearly all of those championing a biophilic (see page 6) and natural approach to interior design. This means following the natural rhythms of daylight and designing your home to work with the movement of light throughout the day. A study in 2017 (see page 187) found a direct link between exposure to natural daylight and improved quality of nighttime sleep.

In this chapter, we'll look at ways of designing your home around natural light, how to mimic and support circadian rhythms (see opposite), and how to supplement natural light sources with good artificial light. We'll also look at how to recreate the gentle flicker of candlelight and firelight after sunset. This in turn should help us sleep better, live better and 'reset' our wild body clocks.

We'll also look at the importance of the dark, how to bring starlight and dark skies into your home to help support your rest time, and how to protect the wild world outside your door.

WHAT IS A CIRCADIAN RHYTHM?

A circadian rhythm is our natural, internal body clock. It regulates our sleep, waking and eating patterns and repeats roughly every 24 hours. Although this rhythm is affected by several different factors, light has a big impact on it. Up until a few hundred years ago humans still lived much of their day according to the rising and setting of the sun. Dawn was our call to wake and dusk our signal to rest. In the summer months when days were longer, we got more work done. And in the autumn and winter, as the days became shorter we rested and recovered, supplementing daylight with firelight when required.

Our bodies are still controlled by these same circadian rhythms which tell us when to wake up and when to sleep, but because many of us now live and work indoors, in buildings with limited natural light, we compensate with artificial lights. This, combined with using computers, phones and screens late into the evening, can disrupt these natural rhythms and allow us to stay awake long past our natural sleep time, disturbing our natural sleep patterns and impacting on our quality of life. In fact, disrupted circadian rhythms have been directly linked to poor physical and mental health, with a UK study in 2018 (see page 187) finding that disruptions to circadian rhythms were 'a core feature of mood disorders'.

Designing the layout of your home according to how the light moves around a space is the first thing to consider when trying to tune your body back into receiving these natural light cues. Positioning yourself near a window as often as possible when indoors will increase the amount of natural light you absorb, and the colour of light at different times of the day will tell your body to either wake up or wind down. The following project shows how to create a light map and how to use this as the basis of your decorating decisions.

PROJECT

How to make a light map

So often when we move into a new home, particularly if it's a small space or a rented home, the floor plan is fixed and we adapt to the layout given to us. If a floor plan dictates that one space is a bedroom and another is a living room, then we follow that plan. But it's worth giving this some careful thought, because where a developer or architect places a bedroom doesn't mean it's necessarily the best place for maximizing the levels of light that enter each room.

The ideal layout for a home is one that follows the way a light changes throughout the day. For example, rooms that face east, where the sun rises, should be used in the morning, and rooms that face west, where the sun sets, should be used in the afternoon and evening. In the northern hemisphere, south-facing rooms that get midday and afternoon sun should be used during the bulk of the day and north-facing spaces might be best utilized after dark (in the southern hemisphere, this is reversed). By using the space in this way, you are exposing yourself to the correct type of natural light at each stage in the day (bright and cool in the morning, warm and diffused in the evening).

While it's not going to be practical for many of us to change the layout of our homes totally, there are still small ways to tweak any space in order to follow the light around more effectively and increase your exposure to natural light throughout the day. Creating a light map is the first step to achieving this.

NORTH, SOUTH, EAST OR WEST?

Draw or print out a floor plan of your home and mark on it which way each room faces. Most smartphones have an inbuilt compass that can help with this. Label each side north, south, east or west and then work out which rooms fall into each category. The aim is to see if your home naturally has a wild aspect, or if you could make some adjustments to allow you to follow the light around your house as the day progresses. Take a look at how you currently use your space and see if there are any small changes you can make to help tweak your layout to fit the time of day. Ideally you want to maximize your exposure to bright morning sunlight first thing and softer evening light from late afternoon onwards.

East-facing rooms get:

Bright light first thing in the morning

They are perfect for:
- Bathrooms
- Bedrooms
- Breakfast spaces

Tweak your space

If you can get ready for work in an east-facing room, you'll get the benefit of the clear, bright morning sun, helping you to charge up for the day ahead. If you don't have an east-facing bedroom, maybe you could move a mirror and dressing table into the corner of an east-facing room so you have somewhere bright and sunny to get ready in the morning. Alternatively, could you find somewhere east-facing to sit with a morning cup of tea or to eat breakfast? The closer you can get to a window the better.

West-facing rooms get:

Warm afternoon sun

They are perfect for:
- Family rooms that are used in the afternoon/evening
- Wind-down areas

Tweak your space

As the sun travels from east to west throughout the course of the day, the light levels in a west-facing room will be optimum in the afternoon and the sunlight will have a golden warmth to it. If you are at home in the early afternoon, see if you can spend some time in a west-facing room to soak up some of this mellow sunlight. If you work from home, simply taking your laptop to work in a west-facing space would help you to do this, or if you are at home with children perhaps you could set up a children's play area or homework station in a room with a westerly aspect for some of the afternoon.

South-facing rooms get:

Direct sunlight for the longest amount of time during the day in the northern hemisphere (in the southern hemisphere, this would apply to north-facing rooms).

They are perfect for:
- Family spaces that are used a lot during the day
- Growing indoor plants that need high light levels
- Working from home

Tweak your space

See if you can create a south-facing space to spend some time in during the middle of the day, as this will increase the amount of clear, direct daylight to which you are exposed. South-facing rooms get the strongest levels of sunlight for the longest amount of time, so these spaces should be prioritized for everyday tasks where possible. Home working, home schooling and children's play will all benefit from a south-facing aspect, although you will need to provide a bit of shade if you're working on a computer or at a desk, as the light contrasts will be strongest in this space.

North-facing rooms get:

Lower direct light levels than any other type of room in the northern hemisphere (in the southern hemisphere, this would apply to south-facing rooms).

They are perfect for:
- Evening rooms to be used after dark, such as TV rooms

Tweak your space

North-facing rooms get the lowest levels of direct sunlight all day long and will feel cooler as a result. If you have north-facing rooms, explore whether you can borrow some light from other rooms either by opening up dividing walls or through the clever use of mirrors to bring extra light into these spaces. You might also benefit from daylight lightbulbs or biodynamic lighting in these rooms too. Prioritizing these spaces as snug evening rooms for watching TV or relaxing when the sun has gone down is ideal.

MAXIMIZE NATURAL LIGHT SOURCES

Once you've tapped into your home's wild aspect as detailed in this chapter's project, it's time to look at how to increase the amount of natural light flowing into your space. Maximizing daylight levels at home also means that you will use less electric lighting, saving energy and money. Here are a few ways to ensure your home feels warm and bright for as many hours of the day as possible.

ALLOW THE SUN TO TRAVEL NATURALLY THROUGH YOUR HOME

Where possible, take down barriers to open up your living spaces to allow light to flow from one side of the room to another throughout the course of the day. This is particularly important if a room is used for more than one activity, but it should also be combined with small snug corners to create a sense of retreat and security.

While it's not always going to be possible to remove internal walls, you could create the same effect by replacing solid wooden doors with glass-panelled ones, or removing internal doors where they are not required (as long as they are not fire-safety doors). Glass-topped furniture will also allow light to travel through it and can be used to enhance light levels, as well as provide a feeling of space in a small room. Another option may be to fit internal windows within an interior wall, for example between a hallway and a living room, to allow light to cross from one space to another.

REFLECT NATURAL LIGHT

Using large mirrors to increase light levels is a simple solution that will instantly magnify a light source, making a real difference to a gloomy room. Place a mirror opposite a light source to reflect it back into the space, or if that's not possible, place it on the adjacent wall as far back as possible, to catch as much direct light as you can. You can also bounce natural light further into a room by using mirrored furniture, such as mirror-topped tables or accessories.

MOVE FURNITURE CLOSER TO LIGHT SOURCES

Position sofas, tables and any areas where you spend a lot of time
as close to windows and light sources as possible. It can be tempting
to tuck a desk into an unused corner of a room for example, but if
there's a way you can place it near or underneath a window you'll
instantly boost the amount of light you get during the working day.
If you can squeeze in a chair near an east-facing window, this will also
help you to charge up for the day while you have breakfast or a coffee
break. Equally, in the afternoon and evening, sitting near a window in
a south- (north, if in southern hemisphere) or west-facing room will
ensure you get exposure to the right type of light to help you relax
and unwind.

CHOOSE COLOURS CAREFULLY

Choose light-reflecting wall colours near to windows and light sources. Bright, reflective tones will catch light and bounce it back into the room as opposed to darker tones that absorb and hold on to the light. Choose satin paint finishes rather than matt if you want to increase the effect and keep ceilings bright as well, to increase the feeling of space. You can also magnify the impact of sunlight by painting the inside of window frames in high gloss paint or, for the brave, a bright yellow shade to really boost the impact of the light flowing in. Dark window frames will obviously have the opposite effect to this, which is worth keeping in mind.

SCATTER THE SUN

Placing reflective décor near a light source will help to scatter and reflect light around a living space and there are so many lovely ways to do this. My favourite trick is to hang something reflective near a window, such as a string of faceted glass droplets or a metallic mobile. As well as sprinkling light around a room, these also bring in natural movement, similar to sitting underneath a tree on a sunny day and watching the play of light as it filters through the leaves. For a more contemporary interior you could choose a mobile of brass discs, simply suspended from slim wires, or for a more whimsical look a ribbon of glass droplets would refract and magnify any light source beautifully.

CHOOSE SUNSHINE-BOOSTING WINDOW TREATMENTS

The first tip here is to keep windowsills clutter-free to enhance light levels. With the exception of houseplants (see page 156), this means sweeping sills clear of picture frames, ornaments and other bits and pieces that can all get in the way of the flow of natural light. Cleaning your windows regularly inside and out will also keep your sunshine levels as high as possible.

Ensure any window treatments sit away from the window if possible (see page 000). This means extending curtain poles past the edges of the window, so curtains can be pulled right back rather than obscuring part of the window and fixing blinds and shades above a window alcove rather than within it. The aim is to keep the full width and height of the window clear and uncluttered to make sure you aren't cutting into your valuable light source.

If you need to screen the lower half of your window or block an urban view, use a window film containing reflective particles rather than dark blinds or curtains. This will work to diffuse any light coming into your room and cast a veil over an unattractive view without totally blocking natural light levels.

BRING LIGHT DOWN FROM ABOVE

To really boost your light levels, consider installing skylights if these are a possibility. While a window will be in shadow for several hours a day, skylights draw down overhead light for a much longer period of time and will help to flood a room with natural light. A recent UK Green Building Council Healthy Homes report states that 'higher level glazing admits significantly more daylight than low level. Therefore, glazing primarily for daylight ought to be as high as possible on the wall (or skylights in the ceiling)'. I consider them to be worth every penny if you are thinking of upgrading your space.

If you're undertaking renovation work, but a full skylight is out of the question, you might want to consider light tunnels as a way to draw down light into a dark room. These are tubes that bring light down from above and are particularly effective in small, dark spaces such as hallways or bathrooms. Light tunnels can be retro-fitted to homes or designed in at planning stage if you are undertaking renovation work.

Light tunnels really can be transformational. I stayed in a cottage in Wales a few years ago that had a tiny, dark bathroom tucked under the eaves with only a very small window. To counterbalance this, a light tunnel had been added right above the shower, which transformed the light levels of the room and meant you could have a shower under a beam of bright natural sunshine every morning.

ARTIFICIAL LIGHT

Once you've maximized all your natural light sources, it's time to supplement them with artificial light. A good home will have a clever mix of the two and each will support the other. Artificial light can actually help to make your home more 'wild', in as much as you can use it to mimic circadian rhythms (see page 129), to help reset your body clock.

Before the invention of artificial light, our ancestors would have extended their working day by using firelight and candlelight after sunset. The gentle flicker of firelight was helpful in aiding rest and relaxation, as well as encouraging conversation and social gathering after dark. Even today, sitting in front of a fire has a soothing and restful effect on the body and mind; in fact, a 2014 study (see page 187) found that gazing at the flickering light of an open fire and listening to crackling sounds had the effect of lowering the blood pressure of participants.

Bringing firelight into your home will undoubtedly provide a link to the wild and the gentle flicker of candlelight or the crackle of an open fire is both soothing and primitive. However, recent research has suggested that unfortunately, lighting fires indoors might actually be damaging to health. A 2020 study (see page 188) into indoor air pollution by The University of Sheffield and The University of Nottingham found that particulate matter was released indoors when participants opened the front of a wood-burning stove to refuel it. While further research into this topic is needed, it would be prudent to consider the effects of burning wood indoors and to do so with caution.

However, we can still learn valuable lessons from our ancestors' use of flickering flames as a light source in the evening – namely that the warm, orange-toned light is both relaxing and soothing after sunset and something we could consider replicating with our use of artificial light sources.

EMBRACE BIODYNAMIC LIGHTING

Biodynamic lighting is where you adjust your light source depending on the time of day and try to mimic natural light, making sure it's bright and cool in the morning and warm and soft in the evenings. While research is still being undertaken into this area, there would seem to be indications using biodynamically adjusted artificial light indoors can have a positive impact on mental health. A 2019 study (see page 188) into the biodynamic lighting effects on the sleep pattern of people with dementia, for example, reported a positive effect on reducing nighttime wakings and daytime sleep.

If you want to experiment with introducing it at home, the basic concept is to use bright, cool lightbulbs for rooms you use in the morning, and soft, warm lightbulbs in rooms you will use in the evening. This is because the naturally blue-toned light of morning sun helps to suppress melatonin production, encouraging us to feel alert and awake, whereas the red-toned light of the evening sun does the opposite and stimulates the production of melatonin, creating a sleepy state. Some rooms such as bedrooms may need a combination of the two (see below).

LAYER YOUR LIGHT SOURCES

Most rooms will need a mix of light sources. Generally, it's a good idea to use bright light for task lighting and softer light for lower level evening lighting. Task lighting includes most ceiling lights, focussed lighting around mirrors or over worksurfaces and in any room you'll be using first thing in the morning. Softer evening lighting can be added in layers at a lower level to any room you'll be using from the afternoon onwards. Use floor lamps and table lamps to create a soft wash of light and a diffused glow. Bedrooms may need cool bright bulbs in overhead lights for getting ready in the morning and softer, warm lightbulbs in bedside lamps for the evening.

CUT DOWN ON YOUR SCREEN TIME

Another way to reset your wild body clock is by reducing your use of digital devices from dusk onwards, or set them to night mode (because blue light from digital devices plays havoc with your natural sleep cycles). Removing screens from bedrooms is ideal, but if you can't bring yourself to do that, try to reduce your use of them and supplement them with analogue pleasures, such as reading a book by the light of a warm-toned bedside lamp.

CREATE WILD REFLECTIONS

You can also use artificial light sources to play with reflections and patterns. A lampshade with a cut-out or printed pattern can cast wild shapes on a wall or table. Leaves, flowers and other natural motifs are all lovely shapes to project onto an indoor surface. Tord Boontje's flower garland light (a leaf and flower garland made of a sheet of copper that can be twisted around a light bulb to throw woodland shadows) is my absolute favourite for this.

EMBRACE THE DARK SIDE

As a counterbalance to encouraging plenty of natural light into your home, it's also important to consider the dark. In order to get enough good rest and to reset our body clocks, we need enough hours of darkness at night to help support this. But thanks to increased outdoor lighting and the urbanization of our planet, light pollution is sharply on the rise. Outside lights can spill over into surrounding areas, chipping away at dark skies, preventing a clear view of the night sky. And it's not just our sleep that's being affected by this; light pollution at night is also having a devastating effect on the wildlife outside our front door by disrupting natural rhythms and confusing nocturnal animals.

REDUCING LIGHT POLLUTION

Kevin Gaston, Professor of Biodiversity and Conservation at the University of Exeter, and his colleagues have undertaken research into the effect of light pollution on the natural world (see page 188). 'Light cycles are fundamental (along with temperature) to organizing the biological world – they drive what we might call the rhythm of life', he explains. When we introduce artificial outdoor lighting at home it can disrupt these cycles, by blurring night and day and affecting the wildlife that rely on these cues.

Outside lighting is common to most houses and apartments; it's practical and useful to help guide the way at night, and it's often used to extend the length of time we can spend outdoors. But there are things we can all do to reduce the impact of it and to lessen the amount of light pollution each household emits. The simple principle to reducing light pollution is to limit lighting to the places and times where it is genuinely needed. Kevin suggests the following steps at home to reduce your impact and create a wilder experience for everyone around you.

1 Remove any outdoor lighting that you don't really need (many houses have outdoor lights for decorative purposes, lights that could be switched on just when they are required, or lights that could be triggered when needed).

2 Limit the spread of light to just where it is required, making sure it is properly shielded and removing uplights.

3 Ensure lights are only on when they are needed, for example, not throughout the night.

4 Avoid using bright white lights wherever possible; lower intensity and narrower spectrum lighting – e.g. less blue light – will almost always be less environmentally damaging.

5 Ensure that indoor lighting spreads outdoors as little as possible, try using curtains, blinds and shades.

And why not take your rewilding a step further by helping to campaign for dark skies in a wider context. Are there any opportunities to help reduce light pollution in public and business spaces near you (e.g. office blocks where lights are left blazing all through the night)? If not, could you start such a venture?

WHY ARE DARK SKIES IMPORTANT?

If you've ever taken a midnight walk and seen the stars glittering above or walked home under the wash of moonlight, you'll know the power and magic the night sky can hold. A dark sky is the equivalent of a pause, a chance to take a deep breath and reset at the end of each day and I would argue that access to dark skies is essential for our mental wellbeing.

One of the most magical and 'wild' houses I've ever stayed in was a tiny stone cottage hidden deep in a Welsh forest, accessible only via a single hairpin road and shrouded deeply by tall, dark trees. When we climbed out of the car and switched off the engine, it was so still you could almost feel the forest breathing. It was wonderful and eerie at the same time – the mark of a truly wild place.

The ground floor rooms of the cottage were dark, cool and still, encased in layers of heavy Welsh stone. Windowsills almost a foot deep framed mountainside views and when we closed the thick wooden door you could almost feel the dark of the trees pressing in on all sides. With the fire lit in the hearth, the house felt secure enough to wait out any passing storm or heavy snowfall.

But when we climbed the small, steep staircase, the top half of the house revealed itself to be another world. Up here it was like being perched in a bird's nest and it seemed as if you could see across the entire rooftop of the soft, still valley. In the bedroom, a large skylight had been positioned over the bed and because the cottage was in a dark sky area, as soon as the sun set over the mountainside a vast patchwork of stars glittered into view through this window. It was so magical that the room needed no other decoration than the glass window into the sky above. We only stayed in that cottage for a couple of nights, but I still think about the magic of that quiet tree-top bedroom with the vast galaxy of stars wheeling overhead and the moon gently washing down into the room.

8

WILD
PLANTS

Houseplants are magic – they're the quickest, cheapest and easiest way to transform your indoor space and keep you connected to the wild while indoors. They come in every shape and size, they can clean the indoor air, boost your happiness levels and many even have medicinal properties.

Caring for houseplants is a very calming and grounding activity, serving as an essential link to a slower pace of life. As long as light levels are high enough for plants to survive, you can create little clusters and pockets of wild throughout your home, from pots to terrariums and hanging planters. You can also bring in herbs, flowers and edibles to weave in even more layers of wild.

At a basic level, most plants will remove CO_2 from the air and replace it with fresh oxygen. Many can remove toxins from the air and also chemicals commonly found in interior furniture, paints and accessories.

As a living organism, plants need light, water and the right humidity levels to thrive, much as we do, and because of this they bring life and movement to a space as they grow, change and evolve. Studies have also shown that plants and flowers can lower blood pressure and heart rate simply by being in close proximity to you, and they've been shown to decrease pain, anxiety and fatigue in hospital patients (see page 188).

In this chapter, we'll look at ways to bring in a host of different plants, from scented to air-cleaning to edibles, along with some ideas on how to style them to suit your home. From quick-grow crops for impatient kids to soul-enriching plants that will add more and more to your happiness each year, there's something to suit every home.

AIR-CLEANING EVERGREENS

In order to survive in our warm, heated homes, most indoor plants are tropicals, suited to hot climates, so they are never going to directly replicate what you can see outside your window unless you live in a tropical environment. But choosing the right plants will allow your home to have evergreen colour all year round, which is especially important in the winter months when the world outside is less colourful. Most houseplants will live and thrive for many years if well nurtured (see below). They can also help to purify indoor air by eliminating toxins, which is why they are my number one décor item for a fresh, natural home. NASA famously researched the benefits of houseplants in the 1980s and their research has set the bar for houseplant use ever since (see page 188). A few of my favourite houseplants, as recommended by NASA for cleaning the air, are:

- Peace lily (*Spathiphyllum*)
- English ivy (*Hedera helix*)
- Boston fern (*Nephrolepsis exaltata*)
- Rubber plant (*Ficus elastica*)
- Weeping fig (*Ficus benjamina*)

HOW TO KEEP THEM HAPPY

There's a popular adage in gardening which is 'right plant, right place'. This simply means you need to find the right location for each plant for it to be happy. If you plant a sun-loving plant in the shade for example, no amount of care will make it thrive, and if you place a moisture-hungry plant in an area of dry sun it won't last long. The same motto can also be applied to indoor plants; if you find the right plant for each location you'll have happy plants. This doesn't have to be tricky – you just need to establish whether your plant needs direct sun, partial shade or indirect sun and find the right spot for it indoors.

You also need to choose your pot with care in order to keep your indoor plants thriving. Nearly all plants need good drainage to stay happy indoors, so whatever pot you choose, ensure it has drainage holes in the bottom and, obviously, a dish to catch the water underneath this. Some decorative pots, such as metal pots on plant stands or woven baskets, won't have drainage, so if you want to choose a decorative, rather than practical, pot, make sure you can place another dish inside it to keep the plant well drained. Most plants dislike sitting with their roots in water, so be sure to empty any standing water regularly.

Taking cuttings and swapping them with friends is a great way to get free plants and you can also pass on your knowledge of the plant's likes and dislikes to give your friends a head start! Then just follow the instructions closely when it comes to watering (which will almost always be less than you are tempted to do, especially in the dormant winter months) and feeding, and refresh the top layer of potting compost periodically.

USE THEM TO LINK INDOORS AND OUT

Placing plants on a windowsill will ensure they get maximum light and warmth, if that's what they need to thrive, but this also has an additional visual benefit. By siting greenery near a window or door, if you also have greenery on the other side of the glass, you're blurring the boundaries between the two and creating the illusion that your home flows seamlessly into the outdoors. This visual trick is lovely for extending the visual sightline out of your house, and for making you feel rooted to and connected with the outside. If you have glass patio doors, try placing a large potted plant at floor level next to the door or hang a planter above a window or door to create a green screen to frame and extend the view.

GREEN UP AN URBAN BALCONY

If you live in a city and have a balcony, plants are a wonderful way to create a little slice of nature above ground level. Even the smallest of balconies should be able to hold one or two plants, and the benefit of a balcony garden is that you can create a real impact with just a few well-chosen pots. With a small area, the key is to use every bit of vertical space – by fixing planters to the balcony railings or by growing plants up the walls you can create a cocooning effect, wrapping your balcony in a cloak of greenery and creating a leafy view from indoors.

There are some specific considerations to address before you start balcony gardening; you'll need to consider the combined weight of plants, pots (plastic pots weigh less than terracotta ones) and soil before overloading the space, and you'll need to think about drainage so your plants don't leak onto the balcony below. But there are so many plants that will thrive on a balcony and bring you much growing (and eating) pleasure.

If you want to create a kitchen garden, you can use the space to grow strawberries, tomatoes and herbs in wall planters. To encourage pollinators and to support local wildlife, you could fill over-railing planters with wildflowers and bee-friendly plants to attract bees and insects. Big leafy plants and tall bamboos can also create a wonderfully lush jungle feel and are excellent for creating a green screen if you need to filter out an unappealing view. Pots filled with spring bulbs can also bring you colour early in the year when it will be most appreciated. For more wild balcony ideas take a look at the chapter on Wild Exteriors (pages 171–185).

SCENTED AND FLOWERING PLANTS

While evergreen houseplants provide a much-needed hit of greenery for your home, you might also want to add a layer of scented plants to bring a wild aroma indoors. Herbs, bulbs and cut flowers will all fill your home with incredible natural fragrance, but will admittedly have a shorter shelf life than houseplants.

MOOD-BOOSTING FLOWERS

Proven to boost our mood, seasonal and native cut flowers are wonderful to bring indoors during their natural growing season. Choosing locally-grown flowers is the best way to be truly connected to your native landscape, rather than choosing flowers that have been flown in from overseas, so check with your florist or online supplier. If you can grow a few of your own flowers to cut and bring in, even better. Cut flowers, admittedly, have a short shelf life indoors but they pack a strong design punch while they last and you can extend their indoor life by looking after them with care. Ensuring they have fresh water (changed daily), cutting the stems at an angle each time you change the water (cutting stems diagonally allows more surface space for them to take up water) and keeping them out of direct sunlight will ensure you get maximum colour and scent from them for as long as possible.

GROW POTTED BULBS

Fresh indoor flowers don't have to finish with the summer though, and indeed during the winter, when contact with the outdoors is limited, having something living and flowering indoors can be a much-needed tonic. To get indoor flowers with a longer life, look for flower bulbs, such as narcissus and hyacinth, that can be grown indoors. These are traditionally grown inside during the winter, where they are 'forced' into flowering earlier than their outdoor counterparts, which won't flower until spring and, as such, they can provide colour and scent in the darker months when both are in short supply. Growing a few of these bulbs in a bowl and placing them somewhere you'll see them every day can really lift a room, and the process of watching them unfold and flower over several days or weeks is absorbing at a time when much of the world outside is in hibernation. Choose richly-scented varieties for maximum wild impact, and pot them up in a large bowl for a centrepiece, or in several small pots to dot around where you'll most appreciate them, such as by the kitchen sink, in a hallway or along a windowsill.

CHOOSE EVERLASTING

While fresh flowers are wonderful to grow and arrange, they do have a carbon footprint that needs to be considered if they are being flown in from abroad, as their footprint will probably outweigh their benefit. But one way of having flowers indoors all year round, without the eco guilt, is to consider dried flowers. A step up from artificial flowers, dried flowers are having a resurgence at the moment and with very good reason; they are cost effective, eco friendly and spectacularly easy to care for. Forget about the dusty displays of the past and think instead of everlasting wreaths, trailing mantelpiece garlands or simple vase arrangements.

EDIBLE INDOOR PLANTS

Nothing tastes better than food you've grown yourself and
often the activity of growing the plant can be as satisfying
as eating the produce.

INDOOR CROPS

Tomatoes and some salad vegetables can all be grown on a sunny
kitchen windowsill or worktop, and an indoor edible garden is a
great project to get kids involved with too. Micro salad crops will
provide a quick hit for beginners as they are speedy, effective and
many will regrow quickly when chopped. Try a mix of leaves
and sow them in succession for fresh greens right through the
growing season.

Cress is another quick-grow classic to get kids involved. Just look for
cress seeds that can be grown indoors, sprinkle them on some damp
cotton wool (absorbent cotton) in a shallow tray, then place in a light
and sunny position and wait for the seeds to germinate. Cress can
also be grown in a tray of potting compost.

Tomatoes will take a little longer to nurture, but you'll get much
pleasure from the growing process. If you've ever walked into
a greenhouse full of tomatoes, you'll know the distinctive smell of
a fresh tomato leaf, with its fresh, spicy warmth and undeniable
'outdoorsy' connection. Look for smaller varieties that are designed
to be cultivated indoors for a faster and more space-efficient
indoor crop.

INDOOR HERBS

Herbs can bring so much life and colour to your windowsill. As
well as adding a visual splash of greenery, they can also provide
flavour for cooking, be used as garnishes for food and drinks, and
release incredible natural scent. Many herbs originate from the
Mediterranean region, so bear in mind they will need lots of heat,
warmth and drainage when considering where to grow them – a
sunny windowsill or kitchen counter is ideal. What you grow will
obviously depend on what you like to cook or drink; some staples

in my house are mint (*Mentha*, as many different flavours as I can squeeze onto my patio), basil (*Ocimum basilicum*), rosemary (*Salvia rosmarinus*) and thyme (*Thymus vulgaris*).

As well as their culinary uses, herbs will also scent your home, bringing in subtle hints of the outdoors, so as well as keeping them in the kitchen, you could dot them around other rooms in your house too. Try placing pots of scented herbs near where you spend time sitting or working to release wild fragrance; a pot or two of a favourite herb on a small table near the sofa in the living room will keep the room fresh, or a small planter on a desk will bring a breath of fresh air into your work space, particularly if you use bright, zingy herbs such as mint or lemon balm (*Melissa officinalis*).

Many herbs also have medicinal properties, helping with anything from relaxation to digestion. Some, such as mint (*Mentha*), can be cut fresh and brewed into a reviving tea, while others, such as lavender (*Lavandula*) release their fragrance when crushed or dried, providing a soothing and relaxing aroma.

PROJECT

Create an edible indoor garden

Herbs are a classic kitchen windowsill crop for good reason – they need minimal care, provide powerful flavour and scent, and will last well if properly cared for, so they are a great edible plant for your first indoor garden. Professor Alistair Griffiths, RHS Director of Science and Collections, suggests also growing microgreens indoors for a super-quick edible crop. I've listed some simple steps below for both options.

CREATING AN INDOOR HERB GARDEN

Start your edible garden with one or two basic herbs that you know you'll use in cooking and experiment with other varieties as you go. Mint plants, for example, come in several different flavours, from strawberry to chocolate, making them great plants to play with. You can buy herb plants cheaply in garden centres or supermarkets, and they are also easy to divide and share with friends.

■ If your herbs are tightly packed into a small pot when you buy them, transplant them into a bigger pot with drainage holes in the base, add some fresh potting compost underneath and on top and firm them down.

■ You can also divide plants at this stage if they are large enough, by taking them out of their pot, splitting the root ball gently into two or three sections and repotting each one individually. This is a great way to get more plants for your money, especially if you can then swap these with friends.

■ Place a shallow dish underneath each pot to collect water.

■ Place your herbs on a windowsill with plenty of natural daylight, as this will help to prevent leggy plants.

■ Water regularly but don't let plants get waterlogged or allow the pots to sit in water.

■ Harvest leaves regularly – this will encourage new growth – but don't go overboard and remove all the leaves in one go or you'll shock the plant.

CREATING AN INDOOR MICROGREEN GARDEN

Microgreens may sound complicated to grow, but it's really just the fancy name for the seedlings of leafy herbs and plants such as spinach, rocket (arugula) or basil. While you would usually allow these plants to grow to full size, a microgreen crop is harvested at the seedling stage so it provides you with tiny leaves that pack a powerful flavour punch. As they are so quick to grow, you can keep sowing and growing crop after crop.

■ Find a container – you can use anything you have to hand for this: a yogurt pot or ice-cream tub would work.

■ Fill your container with potting compost and plant your seeds according to the packet instructions.

■ Place on a windowsill with plenty of natural sunlight. As these grow so quickly this is important, so pick a nice sunny spot if you can.

■ Water regularly but don't let the compost get waterlogged.

■ As soon as the seedlings appear (a few days later), harvest them and use them to add concentrated flavour to salads and cooking.

■ Sow more seeds to keep your supply going.

HOW TO BRING PLANTS INTO EVERY ROOM

Although there are some obvious places to grow indoor plants, such as kitchen windowsills, I think there's a case for having plants in nearly every room in the house. Here are a few ideas for adding them into each space.

PLANTS IN YOUR OFFICE

Studies have shown that indoor plants can boost creativity, happiness and productivity when used in the workplace (see page 188), so if you have a home office, try to green it up a little. Just bringing in one or two plants where you can see them (right next to your computer screen is ideal) should make a big difference if it encourages you to take a few minutes out of each working day to check them and look after them. I find having a plant just beyond my computer screen is also a useful reminder to look away from the screen for a few minutes every now and again to focus on a different viewpoint and allow the green foliage to give my eyes a much-needed break. Scented herbs are lovely to have in a home office if you need a burst of energy: mint, rosemary or any other zingy herb you love the smell of can give an energy boost and freshen up stale air.

PLANTS IN THE BEDROOM

You have to be a bit careful when keeping plants in a bedroom, as many houseplants reverse their osmosis process at night and instead of releasing oxygen into the air, they start to release carbon dioxide instead. There is a small group of plants, however, who do the opposite and keep releasing oxygen into the air through the night. Pick one of these to have in your bedroom to help you get a good night's sleep.

- Aloe vera (*Aloe barbadensis miller*)
- Dendrobium orchid (*Dendrobium nobile*)
- Gerbera (*Gerbera jamesonii*)
- Peace lily (*Spathiphyllum wallissi*)
- Moth orchid (*Phalaenopsis*)

PLANTS IN THE BATHROOM

Some houseplants love the warm and humid conditions of a bathroom (if light levels are high enough) and I always have one or two leafy plants on my bathroom windowsill and at the end of my bathtub, where they seem to thrive. If space is tight, you could try hanging a small planter from the end of a curtain rail or from a ceiling hook to get your nature fix. As well as houseplants, you could also bring herbs into the bathroom. Some aromatic herbs and leaves release essential oils when exposed to the heat and steam of a bathroom and can liven up your morning shower. For an invigorating wake-up call, try hanging a bunch of cut or dried eucalyptus or rosemary near your shower head (but not so they will get directly wet), run the water and wait for the steam to release a natural burst of fragrance.

9

WILD EXTERIORS

So far we've looked at how to rewild our homes on the inside. But what about the outside of our houses and apartments? By this, I mean the actual exterior shell of our homes.

Imagine if you could directly rewild the outside of your home, wrapping it in greenery and flowers, offering refuge for native wildlife and making it beautiful for your neighbours and passers-by. By using the outside walls of your home (or any outbuildings) to make space for nesting boxes, flowers and even bee hotels, you can bring the natural world amazingly close, reintroduce butterflies, bees and birds to your patch of the world, and perhaps inspire others in your neighbourhood to join in too.

Why is this important? Since the 1930s, we've lost a staggering 97% of all wildlife meadows in the UK (see page 188), and the World Wide Fund for Nature estimates we could also be losing 10,000 wildlife species every year. We are reducing our green spaces at an astonishing rate, by parcelling up and paving over valuable 'real estate' and turning it into homes that hold little, if any, connection to the land we're covering over. By rewilding the exterior of our homes, we can, in some small way, start to redress the balance, by creating homes for wildlife, reintroducing plants and habitats, and weaving an appealing cover of greenery over concrete, brick and steel.

Many of the ideas in this chapter can be adapted for any type of home, but they work especially well for flats or apartments that don't have direct access to a garden. In some cases you might need the approval of the landlord or building maintenance team before fixing anything to the exterior of the building, but many of these ideas are simple, quick and easy and shouldn't cause any problems.

GREEN THE EXTERIOR

Climbing plants are a beautiful and satisfying way to rewild the exterior of your home and they are great at drawing a veil over less-than-attractive exterior features or unappealing brickwork. Choose the right plants and you can also create a tiny wildlife sanctuary. Planted at the foot of a wall, near a door or below a window, climbers such as clematis, rose, jasmine or wisteria will all scramble up and along walls with a bit of help (they'll need something to hold on to, such as trellis or wires) and will cover grey walls with colour in spring and summer. As well as providing a beautiful screen of greenery, climbers can also provide cover for birds and nectar or berries for insects, instantly making your home more appealing to all kinds of wildlife.

You don't need a garden to plant climbers either – you can grow many climbing plants in pots and train them to grow up an apartment wall or even along balcony railings. Because pots can be placed on gravel or flagstones, they are also a good option for greening your exterior if you don't have a planting bed directly outside your home.

HOW TO CHOOSE THE RIGHT CLIMBING PLANT

Whether you want to attract birds, feed pollinators or cloak your house in greenery year-round (or do all three), there's a climber for you. You can choose plants that release scent at night, or those that flower in winter when colour and life is most needed. In fact, if you find you need a midwinter boost, I highly recommend planting something winter flowering if you have the space. When I moved into my current home, there was a scrap of winter-flowering jasmine already planted along the front wall of the house. Throughout spring and summer it produced whiplash shoots of green that caught visitors around their ankles, but although I waited patiently for the flowers, none appeared. And then, on the darkest, muddiest week of the year, when all other colour had faded from the garden, it rewarded me with a burst of tiny flowers – little yellow stars blazing outside my door in the bleak midwinter months, bringing light and life when most needed.

I asked Professor Alistair Griffiths, RHS Director of Science and Collections, for his top climbing plants for the following categories:

Plants for summer colour

- Clematis spp. and cvs. (i.e. various species and cultivars)
- Everlasting pea (*Lathyrus latifolius*)

Plants for winter colour

- Any of the variegated ivies
- Winter jasmine (*Jasminum nudiflorum*)

Berries for birds

- Firethorn (*Pyracantha* 'Orange Glow')
- Honeysuckle (*Lonicera periclymenum*)

Plants for pollinators

- Climbing hydrangea (*Hydrangea anomala* subsp. *petiolaris*)
- Common jasmine (*Jasminum officinale*)

Plants for scent

- Star jasmine (*Trachelospermum jasminoides*)
- Clematis (*Clematis armandii* 'Apple Blossom')

Evergreens for year-round cover

- Ivies
- Californian lilac (*Ceanothus* 'Concha')

Edible plants

- Skinless kiwi fruits (*Actinidia arguta* cvs.)
- Grapevines

WALL-HUNG PLANTERS

If you don't have space for pots, you could try a wall-hung planter as a quick fix. As long as you have easy access to water it, you can plant up herbs, edibles or pollinator-friendly plants (see page 180) and add some instant colour and life to your walls. You can buy planters that attach directly to the wall, or alternatively look for iron rings that fix to the wall into which you can drop a plant pot; these are good for easily switching round plants seasonally and updating your displays. If using wall planters, ensure they have enough drainage and they won't drip onto a balcony or window below.

UPDATE YOUR BASKETS

Although they may have fallen somewhat out of fashion recently, hanging baskets are another option to green up your exterior and they are really easy to update seasonally. I think they look fantastic planted up with trailing edibles such as tomatoes or strawberries, but you could also plant herbs or even sprinkle in a packet of wildflower seeds to create a micro pollinator paradise outside your window or door. Place them near a window so you can admire them from indoors and ensure they also have adequate drainage.

ATTRACT THE BIRDS

Want to see more wildlife in your little patch of the world? Why not bring the birds to you by making the exterior of your home appealing to feathered visitors. To attract birds you need to provide food and preferably a nesting spot, and both of these needs can be met by fixing feeders and nest boxes to your exterior. I asked the RSPB's Wildlife Gardener, and author of RSPB *Gardening for Wildlife*, Adrian Thomas for his advice on how to attract and care for birds outside your home.

CHOOSING A FEEDER

'In terms of how to feed, hanging feeders are undoubtedly the most popular,' says Adrian. To keep the seed or fat dry, choose a feeder inside a perspex tube to help keep the food fresh for longer. If you're worried about squirrels or larger birds stealing all the food, look for feeders with cages over the top to deter them. Adrian also recommends spring weighted feeders, as these are designed to close under the weight of anything larger than small birds.

If you don't have space to hang a bird feeder, you can attach a feeder directly to your window. These simply attach to the glass with clear suckers, then all you need to do is fill them with seed and wait for the birds to appear. They are brilliant for watching the birds from a cosy seat indoors and are the perfect option when wall space is limited. Worried about birds flying into a window? Don't be. According to Adrian, research has shown that window feeders can actually be safer than if the feeders were a short distance away from the glass. The reason for this, he explains, is that if a bird is startled at a window feeder and flies into the glass it hasn't had time to build up momentum. It's also more likely to be aware of its reflection in the first place, he adds, and avoid a collision.

Just remember that birds do like to approach feeders step by step. 'They don't tend to wing in from a distance straight onto the food as they like to work out whether it is safe before they do,' says Adrian. If your feeder is on a balcony, or doesn't have any trees or bushes nearby for cover, you might struggle to get many visitors, so to counter this try greening up your exterior or balcony (see pages 173–174) to create those essential stepping stones.

WHEN AND WHAT TO FEED

Food is essential in the winter months, but Adrian also recommends feeding birds all year round. 'During summer, the amount eaten is likely to drop as birds take advantage of nature's bounty, so adjust how much food you put out – you don't want piles of it sitting uneaten. But understand that actually the "hungry gap" for many birds is in spring when the natural supplies have been used up, no plants are seeding, there are few insects on the wing, yet garden birds face all the demands of setting up territory, finding a mate, making a nest and laying eggs.'

When it comes to the food you put out, Adrian recommends 'fast foods' which means things that birds can eat quickly. He recommends sunflower hearts, which are the soft inside of the sunflower seed, or bite-sized lumps of fat, as well as mealworms for a fast, energy-rich snack. He also recommends buying good-quality food wherever possible, in order to have better success; some of the cheaper bird foods, he explains, are filled out with inexpensive grains, such as wheat, that won't attract much to your garden other than pigeons. If possible, buying your bird food from wildlife charities will also ensure any profits to go straight back into wildlife conservation.

KEEP IT CLEAN

'Perhaps the most important thing when feeding birds is to pay as much attention to the hygiene around your feeders as to the feeding itself,' says Adrian. 'Clean out feeders on a regular basis, using a weak disinfectant solution and then rinse the feeders thoroughly in clean water and let them dry out completely before refilling.'

Birds also need water year-round to drink and bathe in, so if you have a balcony or terrace, see if you can squeeze in a water dish for them too. Keep it refilled during hot weather and ice-free in winter.

BIRD BOXES

A simple bird box attached to a sheltered spot on an exterior wall will instantly make your home more wildlife friendly. If you want to attract different types of garden birds, there are varying styles of box available specifically designed for different species.

Bird boxes can be put on exterior walls and, for some birds, such as starlings and house sparrows, they are more likely to be used than if they were in a tree explains Adrian. Swifts and house martins are also attracted to houses, so he advises putting up swift boxes (or even better, having integral swift bricks fitted) and house martin cups for these. If you live in a high-rise building, you're actually more likely to get swifts or house martins visit, he adds, as their nests need to be about 5m (16ft) up, and under the eaves, and they also need a clear flight line in. He also stresses the importance of providing nesting sites, as he explains that numbers of all these four species have declined considerably in recent years. By providing them with nesting sites, you can help to turn around those declines.

WHERE TO POSITION A NEST BOX

Nest boxes need to face between north and east [in the northern hemisphere], so that they don't get too much sun or face directly into the wind and rain, explains Adrian. If this isn't possible, he says, you might get away with swift boxes and house martin cups facing other directions, as long as there is a large overhang of the roof to provide shelter. Height is important too and he advises that house sparrow and starling nest boxes can be put anywhere from 2.4–6m (8–20ft) up a house wall, he warns that putting them any higher could reduce chances of success. Climbing plants can also provide shelter for small birds too, and if you have a wall with climbing plant cover, Adrian suggests tucking an open-fronted nest box in behind them for robins or even pied wagtails.

PROVIDE GREEN SHELTER

Adrian agrees that greening up your exterior (see page 173) is a key part of encouraging wildlife. 'If you think that birds (and indeed most of nature) thrive where there are plants, then you can see why most house walls are a desert for wildlife. It is great that we can use these bare man-made cliffs to offer nesting sites for birds, but just as important is greening up those walls. If you have the chance to grow climbers up a wall, or indeed grow trailing plants over a balcony, then you are doing a wonderful job of giving life to a dead space. The greenery will offer shelter for birds, but also cover for insects that the birds can feed on. Some climbers also have nectar and pollen, and then berries. Yes, we always need to be mindful of the aerial roots that some plants use to cling to walls as aerial roots can damage brickwork by loosening the pointing, but there are some wonderful ones to try (see page 174). A good climber will also help insulate your house from summer sun and winter cold, so get it right and it's a win-win for you and for wildlife.'

CREATE A HOME FOR POLLINATORS

We are all becoming so much more aware of the importance of bees and pollinating insects to the wider ecosystem and as our awareness grows, so does the urgent need to support and protect them. The first step to bringing bees, butterflies and other pollinators up close to your home is just the same as with attracting birds – you need to provide food and shelter. Pollen-rich plants will supply the former, and can be provided for them either in pots, climbers or a window box. Try lavender (*Lavandula*), borage (*Borago officinalis*), scabious (*Scabiosa*), ox-eye daisies (*Leucanthemum vulgare*) or verbena (*Verbena*) in window boxes, and choose jasmine (*Trachelospermum jasminoides*), hydrangea (*Hydrangea petiolaris*) or single-flower roses (*Rosa*) for climbers. Once you've attracted them, you can then add a bee house or insect hotel to provide a safe place for insects to overwinter, to nest and lay their eggs. As well as traditional 'bee hotels', you can also buy 'bee bricks', which are regular-sized masonry bricks with several little holes drilled into them for nesting bees. These bricks can be used in any new building or exterior wall to provide an integrated bee home.

GREEN YOUR ROOF

It's not just walls and windows that can be rewilded – the roof above your head could also potentially be given a green makeover. If you have a flat or gently-sloping roof with sufficient structural strength, adding a green roof could be an amazing way to clothe your home in flowers, grasses and life. But if this isn't an option, there are several other ways to create a mini green roof – any garden structure with a flat or slightly sloped roof could be given a wild makeover. Sheds, bike cupboards or even bin stores are great candidates for a mini green roof. Not only will this increase biodiversity and attract pollinators and wildlife, it'll also draw a wild veil over any unattractive features in your garden.

PROJECT

Create a micro wildflower meadow

The UK has lost 97% of its wildflower meadows since the 1930s, so creating your own mini meadow, whatever its size, could help to reintroduce a little slice of this missing colour and biodiversity. You don't need acres of ground space to bring wildflowers back – with just one window box and a packet of wildflower seeds you can create a mini meadow and start to bring the outside of your home to life. While your little pocket of wild might be small, if every house or apartment in your area did the same, they'd join up to create a wild, beautiful patchwork of colour and life. See if there are any initiatives to help green up your street or area or start your own by sharing seeds and ideas with neighbours and friends. Some streets and local councils might also have funds available for greening up the area.

I asked Isabelle Palmer, author of *Modern Container Gardening*, to share her tips on how to create a micro wildflower meadow.

1 Choose your meadow container

Pick the biggest pot you can! There are a few reasons for this, explains Isabelle – you want to give your plants as much room to thrive, this will also ensure you have less watering and they also create more visual impact. 'Using big statement pots gives you a real focal point whether your space is large or small. The downside of using lots of little pots is they make small spaces look cluttered and disjointed.'

There are many different styles of containers available, but Isabelle suggests choosing more modern materials, such as Corten steel, concrete or zinc, which she says will help to complement the plants and the outdoor space. If you have a balcony or a roof garden and are wary of heavy weights she suggests fibreglass planters as a good alternative.

'Terracotta is another lovely material,' says Isabelle, and she recommends styling it to match your space using coloured lime wash paints. She advises choosing as deep a pot as possible and stresses that all pots must have drainage holes in the base of the planter. 'If you don't have this, your planter will become waterlogged and your much-loved display will face an untimely end,' she warns.

2 Choose a pollinator-friendly wildflower mix that will work in a container

'There are some specific seed mixes now for pots and containers, which you can plant out directly into pots in spring,' says Isabelle. These contain plants such as cornflower (*Centaurea cyanus*), marigold (*Tagetes*), poppy (*Papaver*) and yarrow (*Achillea millefolium*), all of which are great for attracting bees and butterflies. The other factor she suggests you consider is position, 'There are specialist mixes for shady areas in case you don't have a sunny position available,' she adds, 'so there is something for every outdoor space.'

3 Provide year-round colour and insect food

'Not only do you need wildflowers, but a mix of perennials are important,' explains Isabelle, 'particularly of the blue/purple colour variety which attract bees and butterflies and will grow year after year.' Perennials can also provide denser vegetation that can shelter birds, bees and butterfly eggs in the winter. Of the blue variety, Isabelle recommends verbena (*Verbena*), lavender (*Lavandula*), salvia (*Salvia*), delphiniums (*Delphinium*), butterfly bush (*Buddleia davidii*) and lupins (*Lupinus*). And to provide vegetation for winter shelter, she suggests ferns, which can create 'colour and shape' in a small space and adds that 'flowers such as sea holly (*Eryngium*) will look good in a winter landscape as they hold their form.'

QUOTED SOURCES

INTRODUCTION

'Urbanization' by Hannah Ritchie and Max Roser, Our World in Data (September 2018, revised November 2019)

ourworldindata.org/urbanization

'Sick building syndrome' National Health Service (22 September 2020)

nhs.uk/conditions/sick-building-syndrome/

'How many species are we losing?' World Wide Fund for Nature

panda.org/discover/our_focus/ biodiversity/biodiversity/

'Everything you ever wanted to know about making and looking after meadows' Plantlife
meadows.plantlife.org.uk/

'The Practice of Biophilic Design – A Simplified Framework' by Stephen R Kellert and Elizabeth F Calabrese

biophilic-design.com/

WILD SHAPES

'Impact of contour on aesthetic judgments and approach-avoidance decisions in architecture' by Oshin Vartanian et al, Proceedings of the National Academy of Sciences of the United States of America, PNAS 110 (Supplement 2) 10446-10453 (18 June 2013)

pnas.org/content/110Supplement_ 2/10446.short

WILD MATERIALS

'Influence of wood wall panels on physiological and psychological responses' by Satoshi Sakuragawa et al, Journal of Wood Science 51(2):136–40 (April 2005)

researchgate.net/publication/226852714 _Influence_of_wood_wall_panels_ on_physiological_and_psychological_ responses

'Interior wood use in classrooms reduces pupils' stress levels' by Christina Kelz et al, 9th Biennial Conference on Environmental Psychology (September 2011)

researchgate.net/publication/326479468_ Interior_wood_use_in_classrooms_ reduces_pupils%27_stress_levels

'Wood in the human environment: restorative properties of wood in the built indoor environment' by David Robert Fell, The University of British Columbia (2010)

open.library.ubc.ca/cIRcle/collections/ ubctheses/24/items/1.0071305

'Council Getting Started Guide –
National Tree Day', Planet Ark,
Make It Wood program

*makeitwood.org/documents/doc-1253-
wood--housing--health--humanity-report-
2015-03-00-final.pdf*

'Health Benefits of Wood' by Think
Wood (2021)

*thinkwood.com/benefits-of-using-wood/
wood-and-well-being*

WILD VIEWS

'View Through a Window May
Influence Recovery from Surgery' by
Roger S Ulrich, Chalmers University of
Technology, Science volume 224, issue
4647 (May 1984)

*researchgate.net/publication/17043718_
View_Through_a_Window_May_
Influence_Recovery_from_Surgery*

'New Methods for Assessing the
Fascinating Nature of Nature
Experiences' by Yannick Joye et al,
Public Library of Science (26 July 2013)

*ncbi.nlm.nih.gov/pmc/articles/
PMC3724873/*

'Anger and Stress: The Role of
Landscape Posters in an Office
Setting' by Byoung-Suk Kweon et
al, Environmental Design Research
Association (May 2008)

*researchgate.net/publication/258132363_
Anger_and_Stress_The_Role_of_
Landscape_Posters_in_an_Office_Setting*

WILD PATTERNS

'Design for Living: The Hidden Nature
of Fractals' by Kim Tingley, LiveScience
(25 January 2014)

*livescience.com/42843-fractals-and-
design.html*

WILD LIGHT

'Linking Light Exposure and Subsequent
Sleep: A Field Polysomnography Study in
Humans' by Emma J Wams et al, Sleep
volume 40, issue 12 (December 2017)

*academic.oup.com/sleep/article/40/12/
zsx165/4439587*

'Association of disrupted circadian
rhythmicity with mood disorders,
subjective wellbeing, and cognitive
function' by Laura M Lyall et al,
The Lancet (15 May 2018)

*thelancet.com/journals/lanpsy/
article/PIIS2215-0366(18)30139-1/
supplemental*

'Healthy Homes Full Report' by UK
Green Building Council (July 2016)

*ukgbc.org/wp-content/uploads/2017/12/
Healthy-Homes-Full-Report.pdf*

'Hearth and campfire influences on
arterial blood pressure: defraying the
costs of the social brain through fireside
relaxation' by Christopher Dana Lynn,
National Library of Medicine
(11 November 2014)

pubmed.ncbi.nlm.nih.gov/25387270/

'Indoor Air Pollution from Residential Stoves: Examining the Flooding of Particulate Matter into Homes during Real-World Use' by Rohit Chakraborty et al, MDPI (7 December 2020)

mdpi.com/2073-4433/11/12/1326/htm

'Health Effects of Biodrynamic Lighting in Clinics' by Wilfried Pohl et al, Proceedings of the European Lighting Conference (September 2017)

researchgate.net/profile/Markus-Canazei/publication/324909027_Health_Effects_of_Biodynamic_Lighting_in_Clinics/links/5aeaa9e8aca2725dabb651b3/Health-Effects-of-Biodynamic-Lighting-in-Clinics.pdf

'Biodynamic lighting effects on the sleep pattern of people with dementia' by Ellen van Lieshout-van Dal et al, Building and Environment volume 150, pages 245–253 (March 2019)

sciencedirect.com/science/article/pii/S0360132319300101

'A meta-analysis of biological impacts on artificial light at night' by Dirk Sanders et al, Nature, Ecology & Evolution volume 5, pages 74–81 (January 2021)

nature.com/articles/s41559-020-01322-x.epdf

WILD PLANTS

'Effects of Flowering and Foliage Plants in Hospital Rooms on Patients Recovering from Abdominal Surgery' by Seong-Hyun Park and Richard H Mattson, American society for Horticultural Science volume 18, issue 4, pages 563–568 (January 2008)

journals.ashs.org/horttech/view/journals/horttech/18/4/article-p563.xml

'Interior Landscape Plants for Indoor Air Pollution Abatement (NASA Study)' by BC Wolverton et al, NASA (15 September 1989)

ntrs.nasa.gov/citations/19930073077

'Office plants boost well-being at work' by Identity Realisation research group, University of Exeter (9 July 2013)

exeter.ac.uk/news/research/title_306119_en.html

WILD EXTERIORS

'How many species are we losing?' World Wide Fund for Nature

wwf.panda.org/discover/our_focus/biodiversity/biodiversity/

'Earth - Why wildflower meadows are so special' by Jeremy Coles, BBC Earth (3 July 2015)

bbc.co.uk/earth/story/20150702-why-meadows-are-worth-saving

WILDLIFE CHARITIES AND REWILDING RESOURCES

Woodland Trust
woodlandtrust.org.uk

The Wildlife Trusts
wildlifetrusts.org

Bumblebee Conservation Trust
bumblebeeconservation.org

The Royal Horticultural Society
rhs.org.uk

Butterfly Conservation
butterfly-conservation.org

The Royal Society for the Protection of Birds
rspb.org.uk

Friends of the Earth
friendsoftheearth.uk

World Wide Fund for Nature
wwf.panda.org

Plantlife
Plantlife.org.uk

Knepp Wildland
knepp.co.uk

International Dark-Sky Association
darksky-org

Star Count
(part of the CPRE, the countryside charity)
www.cpre.org.uk/what-we-care-about/nature-and-landscapes/dark-skies/star-count-2021/

INDEX

ACKNOWLEDGEMENTS

My thanks to everyone at Quadrille for helping to create such a beautiful book. To Sarah Lavelle for seeing the potential and offering me the chance to write it, Stacey Cleworth for her patient editing, Katherine Keeble for the beautiful art direction and Gillian Haslam for her copy-editing skills. I am so grateful to Fiona Lindsay at Limelight Celebrity Management for introducing me to the team and creating this opportunity.

The ideas in this book were shaped by the knowledge and expertise of many design professionals and wildlife experts, and I am so grateful to everyone who took the time to talk to me and share their experience. In particular, my thanks to Kevin Gaston, Cathryn Sanders, Alistair Griffiths, Adrian Thomas and Isabelle Palmer.

Thanks also to Katy Tyndall, Rachel Calder, Natasha Sawkins, Sean Farran and Steve and Julie Parrott for allowing us to photograph this book in your homes and gardens, and special thanks to Emily Dawe for the prop styling and Maria Bell for the beautiful photography.

Managing Director Sarah Lavelle
Editor Stacey Cleworth
Copy-editor Gillian Haslam
Proofreader Catherine Jackson
Art Direction and Design Katherine Keeble
Photographer Maria Bell
Props Stylist Emily Dawe
Head of Production Stephen Lang
Senior Production Controller Katie Jarvis

Published in 2022 by Quadrille,
an imprint of Hardie Grant Publishing
52–54 Southwark Street
London SE1 1UN
quadrille.com

ISBN 9781787136656
Printed in China

MIX
Paper from
responsible sources
FSC™ C020056
FSC
www.fsc.org